CW00704437

SOUL CLEAI

And Energetic Protection

REMOVING NEGATIVE ENERGIES AND ENTITIES, EARTHBOUND AND EXTRATERRESTRIAL

EVA MARQUEZ

Copyright © 2016, 2023 by Eva Marquez

eBook ISBN: 979-8-9883182-0-0

Book ISBN: 979-8-9883182-1-7

Published by Eva Marquez, eBook 2016, Print 2023

This copy is gently reedited from original version 2016 in March 2023

All rights reserved. This material may not be reproduced in whole or in part, stored in a retrieval system, or transmitted in any form or by any means – electronic, mechanical, or other – without permission from Eva Marquez, except as noted below. Up to 300 words may be quoted with proper credit given. Please use the following credit line: A Healer's Guide For Soul Cleansing, Removing Negative Energies and Entities, Earthbound and Extraterrestrial by Eva Marquez, www.EvaMarquez.org

Eva's YouTube channel for free healing, meditations, and spiritual guidance:
Eva Marquez on YouTube

Disclaimer: Names and identifying details have been changed to protect the privacy of individuals. This book is not intended as a substitute for the medical advice of physicians. The reader should regularly consult a physician in matters relating to his/her health and particularly with respect to any symptoms that may require diagnosis or medical attention.

DEDICATION

To my soul family:

I would be lost in this world without you.
I love you with all of my heart and soul!

Acknowledgements

Thanks to:

My family for loving me and believing in me.

To my wonderful friends listed below. You all are angels sent to me from heaven.

Nina Ricker for your encouragement in my writing, countless hours of excellent editing skills and all the writing tips.

Aurora, Omaira and Veronica, for our learning and sharing Saturday mornings and all the inspiration.

Jose J. Miranda (Veronica's husband), you were pulled into helping me with editing without you even agreeing first, but you gave my story a breath of life and smoothed down rough edges.

Danielle Spencer and Tommye Rodrigues for the final editing touches and encouragement.

Ashley Ruiz, for your gift of the art, drawing of Grey alien Loom (chapter 6) and Axiotonal Grid (chapter 10), that are included in this book.

Roos Jongens, for handcrafted artistic drawings, book cover and drawing of spinning points (chapter 6), and your magic.

Table of Contents

PREFACE

GREETINGS, BEAUTIFUL SOULS!

I have encountered numerous individuals experiencing blockages from negative energies or entities during my career. These blockages are not visible, tangible, or easy to locate, as they are energy blocks attached to someone's soul. These negative energies prevent the soul from evolving and can manifest in various problems and illnesses in physical life.

This book aims to help you communicate with your soul, remove blockages, and release negative energy. It also explains the effects of negative energy. It is crucial to understand how negative energy operates so that you can avoid being control by it in the future. The knowledge will enable you to reclaim your soul energy. During energy work, the process of gathering lost soul fragments (reclaiming) after a traumatic event is known as soul retrieval.

I like to share that this book, which I like to call healer's guide, wasn't written quickly or easily. It took me three years to create with the help of my guides, whom I call the Lights of the Universe. They assisted me in recalling and gathering many of my past experiences, and most importantly, they helped me perfect the techniques to liberate the soul and regain control over one's life. In this book, you will learn about the following:

- Different kinds of negative energy and how to detect/remove it.
- Energy protection for yourself and others
- How to repair extensive damage caused by negative energy.
- How to rehabilitate your energy so you can walk on the Path of Light that you have chosen.

You will gain knowledge about various sources of intelligent negative energy and low-vibration energy:
- Spiritual implants (mechanical implants/parasites of non-human nature)
- Abduction by malevolent extraterrestrials
- Earthbound Spirits (attached entities and spirits that have not crossed over to the other side)
- Past lives (unresolved past lives issues, emotional attachments, and vows from past lives)
- Negative energy from curses and ill wishes

This healer's guide offers easy-to-understand information, energy exercises, and cleansing steps that assume you have basic knowledge of energy work. When I started my spiritual journey, I couldn't afford expensive training, so I learned from books and my spiritual guides, The Lights of the Universe. That's why I'm sharing my knowledge in this book with anyone interested so that you can free yourself and create a life filled with love and happiness. Keep in mind that we all have a unique purpose. Thank you for being here and believing in yourself! I wish you many blessings on your journey.

Love and Light from my heart to yours,
Eva Marquez

PART I

GAINING KNOWLEDGE

CHAPTER 1

GREAT SHIFT

Introductory Teaching by the Lights of the Universe

The Akashic record states that a soul call went through the Universe to star beings willing to return to Earth. The Earth was entering an exciting phase of several significant energy shifts that would allow her children to enter a higher dimension and enable starseeds to awaken their soul memories. Star beings had been coming to Earth since its beginning time in Lemuria. Now once again, they have been called to assist during these changes. They knew the journey could be treacherous as they had to embody human vessels, lower their vibration, and temporarily forget who they were. They knew that the only way to remember would be by overcoming significant suffering in human life and many mysterious illnesses or misalignments. They predicted this would push them to the edge, where they would jump off the cliff into the unknown and realize they had wings to fly and the power to heal. They would remember that they were not left on Earth to suffer because they came there to assist during the great evolution shift. Everything they needed to accomplish their mission was already encoded within them.

And as the Earth entered these energy shifts, YOU answered the call. These powerful energy changes are expected to bring a soul family reunion. The benevolent beings of light created several galactic teams to join with their starseeds on Earth. We, the Pleiadians, welcome you to meet members of our council, The Lights of the Universe, benevolent beings from various star nations who share the same wisdom and intentions. Together and with the aid of this book, we will assist you on your journey if you wish to continue.

In your history are recorded prophecies and stories told by tribal elders of pivotal historical moments. Astrological readings, the Mayan calendar, and other tangible findings support these stories and predictions as accurate.

Awakened starseeds led to this ancient knowledge begin to ride these energy waves, hoping to be a conscious part of these powerful energy shifts. They fill Mother Earth with unconditional love. They assist all willing souls in opening their human hearts and aid humanity in creating a peaceful, joyful, and loving New Earth.

What does it mean for you? Upon awakening, you start remembering your past and seeing both sides of the energy, positive and negative. You also become consciously aware of how negative energy is blocking your life mission. Then you may realize that you are a healer. You have a mysterious feeling that you are here for a reason. You have been a healer in the past and have that inner calling to become a healer again. That is why you are here. But you need to help yourself first, and through your own experience, you start remembering your ancient knowledge and become a true healer. It is essential to understand everything that has ever happened to you.

You have experienced several of these powerful shifts throughout your life. In your past, there have been years that were simply awful. But what if that particular year, event, or tide was meant to shatter you and your memories on purpose and maybe even wash out that part of life that you no longer need so you could start a new, conscious time of your life. What if it occurred to help you instead of destroying you? What if you planned your awakening in your soul contract before your birth? If this rings true to you, then you may also have designed to find the right moment in your journey for this to occur so that you may understand what is happening to you and learn from it to heal. When one cycle ends, new begin. It is only up to you if history will repeat itself or not.

At the beginning of a new cycle, a cleanup job is unavoidable. When it comes to your personal being, you need to look within your soul and cleanse all the negative energy piled up there.

You may need to look even further into your galactic lives if you have made any contracts with malevolent beings and have been tricked into accepting implants to save someone you cared about (whenever it was one being or a whole colony). Implants dim your soul light dramatically and have control over your soul growth.

At the current time, all living life is going through the next evolution stage. Humans have an excellent opportunity to evolve beyond the five basic senses. It is a natural step in evolution that enables you to connect with the higher dimensions and learn who you truly are.

Everyone is experiencing these changes. However, those not tuned in with their spiritual-light bodies are unaware of what is happening to them. They just feel uncomfortably different and confused. Some may behave in other manners than usual.

Then we see those who consciously start working with their light – bodies. They align their mind, body, and souls, yet some are too scared to talk freely about it because they fear being ridiculed. They suddenly feel they no longer fit into society and the life they painfully built.

Then some are afraid to feel with their human heart. They are so scared to acknowledge that maybe they were wrong, failed or made mistakes in the past, so instead, they turn toward anger and violence. They don't understand that they need to clearly see their past to heal it, and only then will they be ready to fully embrace changes and start living a much better life.

We are showering you with unconditional love every second of your life. We would like you to finally notice it and accept it. Allow yourself to be loved. We have not deserted you. We must wait until you connect with us of your free will. The goal of this book is to awaken the ancient healer within you. Instead of telling you stories you may have heard before, we will shower you with the highest vibrational frequency and give you exercises we call tools. We give you these special tools so that you may add them to your "healer's toolbox" and use them to help yourself and others.

RELEASING FEARS

Close your eyes and slowly breathe into your belly. Hold your breath for three seconds and exhale. As you exhale, squeeze all the air out with your belly. Repeat this breathing pattern three times.

Now think about emotions that no longer positively serve you, such as fear, that you want to release.

Take a deep breath and focus on your fear. Allow yourself to feel this fear (or whatever emotion you have chosen to release). Imagine this fear as a heavy block that sits by your feet, weighing you down.

Take deep, full breaths into your belly, and exhale by squeezing your belly. It will feel like breathing in and out through your Solar Plexus. Every time you exhale, imagine this energy block is slowly, effortlessly rising upward in front of your body, starting at your feet, and ending at the top of your head. The blog has a magnetic ability, and as it slowly rises upward, it will collect the fear you hold within (or any emotion you have chosen to release). When you reach the top of your head, take another deep breath, and on exhaling, free this block from its attachment to your body. We will assist you in discarding this energy. Once you let it go, it's gone, just as if an invisible vacuum sucked it all up.

The Lights of the Universe will be delighted to lift this block for you and assist you in an energy exchange. This is especially true with us, the Pleiadians, as we are the soul healers. We will transfer your fear (or old beliefs) into positive energy and use it accordingly for the good. It is just energy. Energy cannot be destroyed but can be transformed. In return, we will fill your soul and your human body with unconditional love to assist you in all changes.

RECHARGING WITH UNCONDITIONAL LOVE

Imagine a bright white light above your head shining down upon you. This light makes you feel calm and peaceful. It makes you feel safe. Now imagine that this light is slowly descending and surrounding you. It is like a warm hug from your soul family. You can breathe this light in and out.

You may experience this light as warm energy pouring into every cell of your body, as a tingling sensation in your hands, or maybe even in your whole body. Allow yourself to feel how much you are loved. Let your soul light shine through your body like sunshine on a bright day.

Use this energy daily to create the goodness you want to share. The integrity, love, and kindness that comes from within touch other souls and heals.

ACTIVATING THE HEALER

Before learning different types of negative energies, we would like to prepare your energy more. We know you are eager to learn and assist others, but it is always a good idea to take one step back, take care of your energy, and then leap three steps forward.

As mentioned above, you prepared for assistance when planning this life. While reading about activation, you will receive an activation if this is your soul's wish. It does not matter if you have received any other healer's attunement, activation, or DNA activation before this. Each energy activation builds upon the energy level you are experiencing and brings you up a bit higher. Light energy does not cause you any harm, and you cannot overdose on this energy, either. It will simply and automatically stop when you have had your fill of the energy needed at the moment. This also applies to your healing energy. You can connect to Universal healing energy while giving energy treatments to yourself, your friends, or your clients. When the body has enough energy, it automatically disconnects.

Let us begin. We are the Lights of the Universe and connected with your guides. Why are my guides already working on transmitting energy, as I have just decided that I would like to accept it? Time is irrelevant to us. You chose to read this book and receive the energy long ago. You may not remember it consciously, but we do. Universal energy allows us to access Akashic memory records. Your guides have access to your memory records as well. That is why when you start consciously meditating and connecting with your guide, your experience increases dreams, astral travel, memory recollection of your previous lives, and memories of special abilities you have used since your creation. Your guides are helping you to remember who you are and what your mission is. They also sometimes allow you to get glimpses of the future. These are called premonitions. There is a reason for each premonition that you have.

Put your hands on your heart and acknowledge your own light, your soul energy which you can feel with each heartbeat. Your soul is a shining light that resides in your heart chakra. Focus on this light and feel its energy. It is the pure and beautiful essence of your being. It is all of who you have been in your past, it is all of who you are today, and it is of who you will be in your future. Your soul is part of the Universe and us, part of you, and part of Earth. Feel unity, serenity, peace, and love. Imagine that your soul's light expands way beyond your body.

Your soul is a part of the soul family that incarnated (at this time) on Earth alongside you. Before you had agreed to come to Earth to assist in her evolution, you had also made plans to meet and reunite with your soul family. The reason for incarnating you and your soul family together is so that you all may assist one another during the awakening or in times of hardship. Each one of you has a particular mission, as well as the ability to help one another. When giving assistance, do not allow others to take advantage of your kindness.

Imagine yourself as a being of light. Set your intention that you are sending the light to your soul family so they can find you. Take a deep breath, and on exhaling, send your light out to your soul family on Earth. Imagine your light expanding in all directions reaching the entire Earth and beyond.

You came here for a reason. Sometimes you may feel lost, and Earth life challenges may bring your energy down. We acknowledge that Earth life is not easy. However, once you begin consciously connecting with your soul family, the challenges you may think are not bearable will become easier. Your story of suffering and healing may help someone else overcome their grief. Your joy and happiness may inspire others. Your healing, psychic, and other abilities may help others understand themselves.

Shine your soul light to the others like you on Earth so you can find one another. Be the lighthouse for those who are lost.

If you are the one who needs help or is lost, ask that your light finds and connects with the lighthouse. Ask that your soul be united with those there to show you the way and guide you during this lifetime.

If you are lonely and are seeking a soulmate, send your unconditional love to your soulmate so that she (or he) may follow the illuminated energy path to find you.

Be the light that shines out and be ready for your soul family to connect with you. Open yourself to this possibility and welcome them back into your life.

We hear your question, "Why do I have to ask for all this if I have already agreed that I will find help?" By consciously asking for help, you will speed up the energy process in manifesting what you want. Many of you have noticed that time is speeding up and that you can manifest faster than ever, but you need to remember to ask for what you want. You are just assuming that all you need will come without asking. This is very humbling and beautiful, but it is not working. We would like you to learn to work with your guides.

You may think that asking for what you need will interfere with your ego, which may be the ego asking for all this. If the asking comes from your soul (your heart), other souls will respond. If it comes from the ego, then other egos will respond. We encourage your soul to ask for what it needs to make your life experience enjoyable. We are here to assist and help you, as are your guides.

ACCEPTANCE

Acceptance is part of soul growth. It is an essential part of your evolution. It is a growing-up step. To us, it is simple; to you, it may be the biggest obstacle as it may be difficult for you to accept all your past.

Consciously accepting all that has happened to you in this lifetime, good or bad, will enable you to create a better life experience. It will weaken all energy barricades that you have built to protect yourself. It will make you a better healer.

Forgiveness follows up after acceptance.

You need to know what went wrong to accept your past or current situation. You do not need to understand the person who did you wrong or know why it happened. All you need is to acknowledge that it was not right. Then, set your anger aside and do not see yourself as a victim. It is as simple as it sounds. Just acknowledge it and accept it.

If you were the one who had done wrong and now conclude that you want to change your life, then accept and take responsibility for all you have done. You cannot escape it because it will eventually catch up with you. Instead, accept your doing and devise a plan to bring light to this world to balance your karma.

Acceptance does not mean giving up. It means surrendering. It means taking your power back and leaving the past in the past. It does not mean "burn the bridges." It means cleaning them up with love and light so they may shine fully. When you clean up your path, you empower yourself million times.

We can hear you say:" But it was not fair!"

Please know that you have chosen your sufferings and roles before each incarnation. Many of your unpleasant events have led you to your awakening point so that you may begin your Earth mission. Also, know that you can change or alter your pre-destined life by taking steps toward your natural spiritual evolution, embracing your mission, and living your life in love and light. The future is not set in stone.

You have been reincarnated during an inspiring time of change. We (Lights of the Universe) understand that many of you do not like all the symptoms of awakening your consciousness and remembering who you are. We know that remembering all the wrong and pain may overwhelm your nervous system and can temporarily hold you down, causing you depression, anxiety, panic attacks, unhappiness, etc. We see that you are trying to find answers to your problems, so we are assisting you on the energy level to set your energy for global acceptance. Global acceptance starts with each individual working with their own energy and then connecting it with other same-minded evolved individuals, thus creating soul groups.

Many of you currently focus on exploring your past lives and how they have affected your current life. But first, we want you to observe your present life.

- What is it that I need to accept?
- What is it that holds me down?
- Is the energy of my unhappiness as strong as I think it is?
- Do I want to be a victim, or do I want to take my energy and my power back?
- Is it necessary to carry this emotional baggage with me all the time?

This is a time to observe, not to blame anyone for what has happened to you. This is a time to see what is inside of you, what holds you down, and what you can release and let go of.

Do not turn your anger and fear into guilt and guilt into anger and fear. Break the pattern. All past life experiences, joyful or sad, have shaped you into the unique individual you are today.

ACCEPTING YOURSELF

Look into the mirror. Look deep into your own eyes. The eyes are the doorway to the soul-mind consciousness.

See yourself for who you are, not who you were or want to be. Just stop momentarily, look at yourself, and acknowledge who you are. There is no right or wrong. It does not matter if you are rich or poor, healthy, or sick, good or bad. Right now, it is the moment to accept your very own self. It is time to acknowledge the entire journey you have endured until now. Look at yourself and feel good about yourself. You do not need any acceptance from others. You do not need forgiveness at this moment. This moment is about you and realizing how far you have come.

Standing in front of the mirror, looking into your soul, acknowledge that you have reached this moment because all the circumstances of your life, good and bad, had led you here into this moment.

If you are standing there, looking at yourself, hating your life, and your wounds are so deep that nothing makes sense, look again. Look into your eyes. You reached this point in life because you are ready for a change. You are consciously prepared. Now you can create a new reality to change your life pattern and create a much happier one.

Accept your life consciously, in your heart and mind.

Some would say, "forget everything and start all over." We suggest that you accept all that has happened to you and move on. Illuminate your path with love and light instead of burning it. We will work hand in hand with your guides, assist you on an energy level to heal your past, and recharge your future. You have volunteered to come to Earth, and we have volunteered to help you understand your mission, your journey, and your purpose.

Acceptance is just one step. You are the creator of your happiness.

ATLANTEAN SOUL HEALING

When studying to be a healer, realize that you have already practiced all this in Atlantis and many times after. You are an old soul, not a rocky newbie doing this for the first time. All healing techniques available on Earth have first been practiced in Atlantis, and you are tapping into your memories of them. You do not want to just use the Pleiadian techniques or the Arcturian techniques that we use on our home planets because the structure of our body is different than yours. Thus, something other than what works for us in the Pleiades will work for you on Earth. For example, our lungs function differently than yours. This is why we had problems living on Earth for extended periods when we first arrived and why we welcomed genetic modifications of our bodies.

During the time of Atlantis, we, as collective star nations, had developed unique healing techniques which combined Earth and Universal healing energies. This was done to maintain a healthy and thriving body, as the body is the soul's vessel. Without it, the soul could not function on Earth.

When we take you to our spaceships and heal you, we utilize that same energy (Earth and Universal healing energy) to assist you. This energy is like a perfect blend of medicine designed uniquely for you. It just must be applied correctly. After Atlantis was destroyed and thousands of years passed, humanity forgot the art of soul healing and focused only on body healing. We are here now to rekindle that memory within you. The body is the lighthouse, and the soul is the light. If the lighthouse is falling apart, you first have to repair the light so you can see what else needs to be mended.

When a disease manifests in a physical body, in many cases, it could be a soul's cry for help. The physical body is simply a vessel for the soul. Since the soul is invisible to the naked eye, you tend to focus on healing your physical body and forget about your soul.

Thus, the diseases and emotional problems will return like boomerangs until you hear your soul pleading for assistance.

True soul healing originates from within the soul, allowing the soul to grow within the body's consciousness. Same as the saying "true beauty shines from within"; true healing starts within your soul and expands to your physical body.

When an energy healer shines her healing light onto her client, the light comes from her soul that is connected to the Universal healing energy. She and the recipient connect on a soul level. The healing light first enters the soul before descending into the physical body. This healing is based on a soul agreement made by everyone receiving the healing energy before the healing itself. Often these agreements were made before the current incarnation.

In spiritual growth, soul healing is essential to ascension and enlightenment. This part of the work has to be done on Earth in your physical body. In this lifetime or past life, trauma on Earth created soul trauma that can only be healed on Earth. While going through soul healing, you will enter a period of transformation that will gradually change you and move you closer to your original self while still in the physical body. This is the work you want to master if you no longer wish to return to Earth.

How do you achieve this by yourself? By listening to your soul's inner whispers of the essence of your true self and the slow but steady conscious transformation.

Simply imagine your physical body as a vehicle you use for transportation and the choices you can make. Most cars that run on gasoline significantly pollute the Earth, break easily, corrode, their life expectancy is not great, and as they age, they eventually have problem after problem. Now imagine a car running on solar power. Clean, efficient, and with a longer life expectancy without environmental pollution. Your soul is the engine to your body, gasoline represents low vibration energy (shame, guilt, despair, grief, desire, anger, hate, pride), and solar power symbolizes higher vibration energy (trust, willingness, acceptance, forgiveness, understanding, love, joy, peace, and enlightenment) that helps your soul heal and grow. The choice is always yours.

A connection with higher dimensions is always available when caring for your body and soul. When your soul remembers that dimensions can operate on solar power, you are healing your soul. Suddenly, communication with beings of light and telepathy will become natural, and you will rediscover many other natural and beautiful gifts you have been blessed with.

Soul healing opens the door to transformation. Cosmic and spiritual energy is constantly available to all of us. When you reach its frequency, you consciously connect to higher dimensions while still in the physical body. This is a prolonged process. Your guides may communicate with you, or you may find a true teacher on Earth. True teachers are rare to find, but they do exist. Self-spiritual work, discipline, and love will all be your allies on this journey.

While you go through soul healing and transformation, you will re-open a part of yourself that you have consciously forgotten. You may encounter many fears along the way. When this happens, put your hands on your stomach (your 3rd chakra) and feel those fears. You can never forget these fears, but they will not harm you if you know they are there as a memory and see them for what they are. Once you have received conscious knowledge of those fears, imagine yourself in the safest place. Breathe deeply and tell yourself, "I am safe. I am safe. I am safe." Let your thoughts of safety transform those fears into peace and love. All the fears that were there to protect you or warn you are now no longer needed. It is important to send that message to your body and your soul so that they can be released.

What comes next is the surfacing of good memories. These memories manifest themselves in your life as a strong passion for a particular activity, a calling to be a healer, different food choices, or an urge to move to a new location. You will find this familiar and comforting because your soul is reminding you. You have already done it before, perhaps several times.

People often find this part exciting and believe all their problems can be solved in minutes. However, much work still needs to be done until you are in harmony with the Universe. Your past is part of your unique energy and is bountiful with wisdom. At this time, you will start consciously working on your past lives healing process. With the conscious knowledge of your past lives, you can heal scars and bruises on your soul, enrich your current life, and get closer to enlightenment.

We know that when you remember this and transform your life, you will activate the true healer within you. You are a gift to everyone around you. As a healer, you are building a bridge between holistic and modern medicine, and there is no reason why your healing should not be as effective and spectacular as it was during the time of Atlantis.

Remember, you are repeating the cycle. Atlantean energy is awakening in the oceans of the Earth, and it is programmed with ancient knowledge and technology. The question is, will the cycle repeat itself, or will you alter it? This is why the soul call was sent throughout the Universe. And you, brave old soul, have answered that call.

We are honored to walk on the path beside you.
The Lights of the Universe.

CHAPTER 2

THE RULES HAVE CHANGED

The rules have changed! You do not have to suffer anymore! We live in an exciting time where you can reclaim your soul's energy and memory. I speak of the personal, unique God's Source essence, a spark of light within. Now at this present time, you have a choice that you have never had before. You can release your past and remove any attachments (internal controlling bodily devices and/or negative energy). You have free will to regain your soul memory. You have free will to remember your abilities from your galactic home and your Earth's past lives. Do you not find this fascinating? Best of all, you will be able to heal your own soul! The only obstacle is that negative intelligent energy wants you to believe otherwise. It wants you to be scared, paranoid, sick, and unhappy to keep control over you.

Help is available. It always has been, and it is here. You may have failed to see it; now it is time to recognize it.

The first step toward cleansing your soul and regaining your energy is to reflect on your life, then consciously understand and accept who you are inside. It has to come from each one of us individually. You must acknowledge without judgment what your past was and what good and bad deeds you have committed in your current life. After healing yourself, you may awaken a deep desire to be a healer to others. This is a sign that you answered a call to join the "Galactic Rescue Team" on Earth.

Conscious understanding and acceptance are the first keys.

If you are ready to consciously acknowledge all parts of your past and make peace with them now in the present, then you are prepared to move forward toward the future. Remember that you are a healer whether you choose to help just yourself or decide to use your unique ability and energy to help others. Most amazing healers had to first heal extensively from the damaging effects of negative energy in their own lives. This is a natural part of the learning experience. You may call it a test. A test on how difficult it is to be functional in a hostile environment and how to overcome it. Can you master this? You should realize that although no one has to suffer, suffering energies may be necessary to activate and awaken your ancient self and release the power deep inside you of which you may not even be aware. Do you know how magnificent you are?

Overcoming negative situations and cleansing negative energies from your life teaches you that you can overcome anything if you have faith and strive toward the light (which I will explain in greater detail as you read on), even if you cannot always see it. It is also important to realize that you, your higher self, carefully designed all these "unhappy, painful, and difficult" life lessons long before your birth. And it is you who can reverse that.

Once you understand that negative energy is just energy that can be dealt with, then you can change your life for the better. You will evolve, and when you are ready, you may feel a calling to serve as a healer to assist others. Life is a gift! Help others to see and appreciate it! Help them understand that we all came here to Earth for a reason.

CHAPTER 3

NEGATIVE ENERGY

There are two basic kinds of negative energy, neither of which serves positively:
- Low Vibration Energy
- Intelligent Negative Energy

Negative energy makes you feel angry, depressed, confused, sad, hateful, greedy, manipulative, judgmental, fearful, and jealous. It fills you with low self-esteem and leads to addictions and self-destructive behavior. It makes you feel miserable most of the time. It will also lead to many mental and health issues, such as depression, anxiety, and possibly more severe physical illnesses. Left untreated, it will cause unbalance in your whole being. The direct effect of this energy is that it holds you back.

Consequently, it holds your soul back. You literally become its slave. It does not want you to progress and shine your light—the light we all possess but do not know how to use. The less you progress, the easier you are to control and the less likely you will be able to help others. It also creates situations so that you will be unhappy and isolated from others because it wants to have you and your energy all to itself. Negative energy is a parasite and will feed off your fears. It is detrimental to your mental and physical health.

If you feel there is something that is holding you back from living a happy life, being in a loving relationship, having a job that you like, doing what it is that you want to do, or if you are depressed or seriously ill and/or most of your endeavors result in failure, you may require soul cleansing. You may do this yourself if you understand energy work; otherwise, seek a qualified, trustworthy healer.

However, before concluding about negative energy affecting you, you must carefully observe it and your behavior/personality pattern. You need to look for the "signs" (which I will explain in greater detail as you read on). You need to ask the right questions: Is your ego causing the blockage, or are you being influenced by negative energy? For example, many people have confided in me that they have worked so hard their entire lives, then when they are almost ready to reach the point of happiness, something unfortunate happens, and they need to start all over again. This pattern usually repeats itself in their life for many years.

There may be two reasons for this happening. The first reason may be that they need to be on their highest path, and their achievements must align with their life's purpose. Ego may be to blame for this. In this case, spiritual counseling, past life reading, healing, and reflection on current life events would be appropriate. The second reason may be that they are being held back by negative energy that is not allowing them to fulfill their life's mission. People who fall into the second category are energy-gifted, or you may also know them as old souls, lightworkers, or starseeds (different names for the same type of person). These individuals have a unique mission, even if they are unaware of it. They are gifted with extraordinary energy and abilities. These souls are most susceptible to psychic attacks and all sources of negative energy.

CHAPTER 4

IMPORTANCE OF ENERGY PROTECTION

The first step in learning about negative energy is knowing about protection. Energy protection and cleansing techniques should be taught to everyone. Once you learn to always keep your vibrations high and shine your soul light bright, you may not require any energy protection tool I will describe. It is always optional, and I want you to know all the options instead of being afraid.

As a healer, when you assist others in removing negative energy of any kind, most likely, its force will personally attack you before you begin the healing. When I began working with my clients to remove negative energy, I felt a negative hit one or two days before the appointment. At first, this perplexed me, but then I began to see a pattern. Not only did it affect me directly, but it also affected my family indirectly. Fortunately, I realized this soon enough and made the necessary adjustments and corrections accordingly. Furthermore, I also experienced a negative energy hit immediately after performing the cleansing attunement on my clients. I learned that negative energy was mad at me because I had separated it from its vessel (my client).

It is good to be prepared because the most vicious attack you will experience will come from non-human parasites. On the one hand, this is a good sign, as you know you have done something good; however, it is unpleasant and will drain your energy. I am not writing this to scare you but rather to inform and prepare you. When you turn the light on in complete darkness, you will realize there is nothing to fear. Your everyday life improves when you know how to protect and cleanse your energy.

I have come across people asking me, "If the Universe gives you the gift of removing negative energy, why does it not give you the ultimate protection?" The answer is easy: "Can you learn to walk without first falling?" Energy cleansing is an ancient skill; you only need to remember and practice the steps to gain confidence. Therefore, the more you learn, practice, and research, the more you remember. In the meantime, you can use various protection tools until you remember that you have ultimate protection within and do not need anything else. Once you learn to always keep your vibrations high and shine your soul light bright, you may not require any energy protection. You will know all the steps.

When I started to work on cleansing negative energy, I was already an experienced healer and thought I knew a lot about protecting myself with my routine. I bet my guides were laughing at me for how naive I was. Well, I was about to learn a fundamental lesson.

Before we proceed, I want to share with you that my knowledge comes from memories awakened by my guides, the Lights of the Universe, at the right time. The Lights of the Universe are beings of light from various galactic star systems. They are my guides and my teachers and will also be your guides as you read this book. They will join with your guides and assist you in finding a unique and personal approach to the teachings and knowledge within this book.

At this moment, you can sense their joined energy. This combined energy will always be with you when you read and study this book, but only if you allow it to stay. If not, then you must ask them to leave. All beings of light follow and respect the Earth's free will law. If there is a being with you, an energy that tells you otherwise, then it is time to re-evaluate this energy's origin and true intentions. It may be different from your best interest.

OPEN AND CLOSE YOUR ENERGY

If there is only one tool that I could teach you, it would be how to open and close your own energy — your personal energy field. Sadly, many energy-gifted people do not know about this basic energy technique. It is so simple, yet so important. Believe me, you will feel so much different when you start using it!

You will learn that I repeat this often if you follow my work.

Many people are obsessed with their physical appearance (both facial and bodily) because it is what is visible to others. If there is some noticeable abnormality, they will go to great lengths to correct and/or eliminate it. We care about how our face looks, how our hair is styled, the shape of our bodies, what we wear, and so forth. But do we care about our energy? No, we do not. Now, let me talk about that non-visible part of us. Just because you cannot see it does not mean you can ignore it. You can sense something wrong; although you may not understand it, you can perceive it. Energy communicates with us in its own way. It can be your best friend or worst enemy, depending on your understanding and perception.

Every energy-gifted person is an empath. An empath's energy acts like a powerful sponge absorbing all energies around it. You unwillingly and unknowingly sponge energy by always keeping your empathic energy field open and unprotected. If that energy is negative (and there is a lot of negative energy all around us), it will adversely affect your body's energy, primarily your mental and spiritual well-being. So why not learn to be consciously in control.

Opening and closing your energy can be compared to opening and closing the front door of your house. For example, You have a party and invite all your friends and acquaintances into your home. You open your front door and let them all in. You all have a great time. Then, after everyone leaves, you close your door and ensure it is locked so that no one can come back to violate your privacy. But imagine what would happen if you were to leave your door wide open after everyone left. How disastrous could that possibly be! What kind of undesirable people would come to "visit" your house? The same goes for your energy. When your energy is always open, you invite anyone (and anything) in. When you close it, however, you are closing the door to your personal energy system and can enjoy the serenity of your own essence. I cannot stress enough how important it is to learn and understand that you are energy, and you can be very easily influenced by other energy in either a positive or a negative way.

Learning to open and close your energy also helps to develop your abilities. You will become more sensitive and alert when open and more at peace when closed. Also, when your energy is closed, you have time just for yourself—time to relax and rejuvenate. You have been incarnated to be of service in this lifetime, but you are not expected to be of service 24/7. As you take care of others, it is crucial to take care of yourself first.

Instruction for opening yourself to energy: 1-2-3

When opening your energy, think of it as activating yourself. Conversely, when closing it, you deactivate yourself, as though placing yourself in sleep mode. To open your energy, you must:

1, Have an intention and/or purpose for your goal.
2, Have an activating code.
3, Switch on your light.

1, Have an intention and/or purpose of what you want to do now- open your energy and getting started.

Opening yourself to energy is very simple. You must realize that every thought is energy. You need to use your willful intentions! Ask to be able to channel, connect with the other side, heal, or just meditate. You can open your energy for yourself or to help serve others.

2, Have an activating code—a personal prayer, saying, symbol, or signature energy imprint (feeling).

Here is an example. You can vary the words depending on the intent of the session. Modify the words that suit you at a specific time. Some people may like to envision a symbol or have a special feeling in their body before the session with which they associate at the beginning of every session. I prefer to say a prayer.

Prayer/Intent

"Infinite Intelligence (God's Source, Creator, etc.), I am grateful to be your clear and open channel for the highest available beings of Love and Light who would like to connect and work with me today. I also thank and ask you, my guide (s) [say the name(s) of your guide (s) aloud if you know it/them, or just think about them], to connect with me at this time and assist me on my spiritual journey and in my spiritual growth. I appreciate the protection I know I am already receiving from you and will continue to receive. Thank you, thank you, thank you."

You can ask for anything that strengthens your connection and activates your highest ability. You must be clear about what you are asking for—whatever it is on which you are focusing during a particular session, whether it is for your own benefit or if you are assisting others. Also, remember to always ask and give thanks for what you desire.

After consciously activating (opening) your energy, you may feel tingling in your hands as your energy vibrates throughout your entire body.

3, Switch on your light internally.

This is the fun part!!! Imagine that you are a light chandelier with a dimmer switch to your light. Now it is time to turn your light on. Picture your chakras from the bottom to the top. Switch on the light in each chakra. Start with your Root chakra, Sacral chakra, and move upward until the crown chakra. As you travel upward, imagine that your chakras illuminate with the most brilliant colors and that each chakra feeds into the other. When you are done, shine your rainbow light outward and imagine it expanding from within your body and then illuminating out of your body. You are now a brilliant, bright rainbow light, and your energy field expands outward, reaching other dimensions.

At this time, you may also express gratitude to all who work with you from the Love and Light family. Now you are ready to begin.

Instruction for closing yourself to energy: 1-2-3

To close your energy, you must:
1, Have the intention to close.
2, Thank your guides and close the connection.
3, Switch off your light.

1, Have the intention to close your energy and finishing.

As you intended to open your energy, now you must plan to close it and bring the session to an end.

2, Thank your guides for their assistance and close the connection.

Express your gratitude to all the beings that worked with you and ask that your connection be closed. Once you are done with your work, close the connection!!! Do not postpone this. Even if you know you will perform another session in a few hours, close the connection immediately unless you are an experienced energy worker. It is also necessary to give your nervous system a break. You can always open yourself to the energy as often as you need it later. I like to say a deactivating gratitude prayer to close the connection.

Prayer of Thanks

"Infinite Intelligence (God's Source, Creator, etc.) and my guide(s) (say the name(s) of your guide (s) aloud if you know it/them, or just think about them), thank you for your assistance at this time, and I ask you to please close our connection for now. Thank you, thank you, thank you."

3, Switch off your light internally.

Visualize your chakras and close them one by one. Switch your dimmer all the way down. Imagine dimming each chakra light while traveling from the Crown chakra downward. You can keep your first and last chakra half open, so you are grounded with Earth and connected with the Divine.

Some people have an easy time using the metaphor of a dimmer. Some like to pretend they have a little door with a lock on each chakra that they can open and close. Do whatever works for you. Also, do not worry about missing an important message when you are closed. If something needs your immediate attention, your guides and other spirits will find a way to alert you, no matter how much you close yourself.

You will not attract unwanted spirits or entities by dimming your light and closing your energy.

When you are finished, you may drink and eat something light to help you ground yourself. The food will kick-start your digestive system and help you regain physical energy.

Note: Learning to open and close personal energy is essential in our evolution. Please teach others the importance of establishing a healthy routine from the beginning!

RAISING YOUR VIBRATION

Raising your vibration is a fantastic personal energy ability that you possess. When your energy is vibrating at a higher level, your DNA also resonates with a higher frequency, making it much more difficult for negative energy to attack you. When you open your energy, you want to keep it vibrating high.

SYMBOL OF LIGHT

There are several ways to raise your vibration. One of them is through "Living Art Energy." The Lights of the Universe have designed a special drawing that vibrates energy called the "Symbol of Light." This symbol combines different colors, shapes, and light codes, raising the viewer's energy vibration.

When you look at this drawing, think of love and unity. Feel peace and serenity in your heart chakra, in your soul. This symbol will directly speak to your soul.

It activates light codes in your thirteen strands of DNA and raises light vibration in the spinning points that feed into your axiatonal lines and raises your vibrations. (You will learn more about spinning points and Axiatonal Lines in the Cleansing Steps.) If you sense any blockage in your body while looking at this symbol, just bring this feeling of blockages up through your upper chakras (pushing the energy upward) and breathe them out into the Universe - as described in an earlier exercise. Call upon your guides to take this energy away from you.

SYMBOL OF LIGHT – MEDITATION

Inhale, take a deep breath, and slowly exhale, releasing all air out. Inhale and exhale, releasing all worries and expectations. Then inhale and exhale one last time.

Imagine a golden light opening just above your head and shining its warm, bright, and beautiful light upon you, filling your aura with this incredible golden light energy and creating a golden column of light around you. You are surrounded by warm and soothing energy. You are safe and relaxed. Inhale the golden light in and allow your whole being to merge with its loving energy. Keep breathing this golden light in and out. Be the light, the love, one with all.

Now imagine in your mind or look directly at the Symbol of Light. Let its energy and impression join your mind, soul, and entire body. Be one with the Symbol of Light.

Spend 5 to 10 minutes in your quiet place with the Symbol of Light. You may feel drawn to the entire symbol or only some part of it. Either way, imagine that you are part of this symbol, and this symbol is part of you. Take a slow, deep full breath; breathe this energy in and out. Repeat as long as you feel it is needed.

Imagine your energy growing and expanding beyond your body. Imagine that your heart chakra, your soul light, is illuminated with the most brilliant light. You may feel tingling and/or spinning sensations throughout your entire body because tiny energy vortexes activate in your body and assist you in raising your vibration.

Continue taking slow, deep, full breaths as you raise your vibration. Feel love, unity, peace, and serenity in your heart, your soul.

The Lights of the Universe recommend that you attune to the Symbol of Light before you start any cleansing sessions by opening your energy system and raising your vibration. You can print a copy and place it in your healing room. You can also take a part of it and/or make your unique Symbol of Light specifically for you. After some practice, you may not need to visualize it at all. You will become one with the symbol and the "soul-raising energy," and merely thinking of it will raise your vibration.

Your Soul Light

Another form of raising your vibration is to shine your soul's light. Sometimes you will find yourself in a situation where there is no time for you to fully open and close your energy. **For example:**
-   You are approached by spirits, energies, extraterrestrial aliens, or guides with which you are not familiar or do not know,
-   You are astral traveling, or
-   You are being taken by extraterrestrial aliens aboard a spaceship.

How will you distinguish between positive and negative energy on the spot? The easiest thing to do is to shine your soul's light.

Some beings are sleek and deceitful. They may pretend to be a deceased family member or one of your guide (s). They will try to convince you they have your best interest for you. Why? They want to steal your energy and take control of you. If something does not feel right when you connect with the energy or your guide (s), follow your gut feeling and test the possibly negative energy. Shining your soul light raises your vibration. Negative energy will not be able to withstand it. Your soul's light will make it feel uncomfortable, and it will leave or ask you to stop. In that case, shine it even more. I cannot even count how often negative energy has tried to deceive me.

I have been under psychic attack numerous times. The one time I was hurt was when the negative energy tried to pretend it was my deceased grandparents. The energy made me believe I was communicating with them, and I could even see and sense their faces. At that exact moment, I also felt that something was odd and not fitting. When I tested the energy, I realized it was not my grandparents. I couldn't believe that I was being tricked. Anyone with loved ones on the other side is susceptible to this negative energy. Remember, it knows and preys on your weaknesses. They see your light and can sense your emotions. Negative energy does not hold your best interests and does not care about you, even as it tries to convince you otherwise. It wants to take your energy and use you as a vessel until you have nothing to give.

SHINING YOUR SOUL LIGHT – ENERGY EXERCISE:

Inhale, take a deep breath, and slowly exhale, releasing all air. Inhale and exhale, releasing all worries and expectations. Then inhale and exhale one last time.

Imagine a bright light inside your chest, in your heart chakra (where your soul sits)

Now imagine your heart chakra gradually growing bigger and bigger. Visualize this with a green, pink, or golden color. When your chakra grows, it will open, and a glorious light will shine. This light illuminates your whole being and shines way beyond your body. Your soul is the center of your Universe, while your Universe is part of the greater Universe. Hence you are part of all that is!

To help you understand this process, imagine a powerful flashlight shining through your being. This is your soul light—this is you. You can do this all by yourself. If you are in doubt or need additional help, call for your guide(s), your soul family. Ask for help, and help will be given to you.

This exercise is a quick and effective solution when encountering unfamiliar energy. You can also use this simple exercise when you find yourself alone with negative people and need a fast change of energy wherever you are. Same, as with your energy field, when you have accomplished what you want to do, then follow up with closing your soul light unless you feel you have evolved to a point where you are not bothered by negative energy, your vibration is high at all times, and you like to keep up your soul light on full blast.

TESTING THE ENERGY

Learning how to test energy is a good idea when you decide to channel beings and work with their energy. I learned this shamanic practice many years ago when I was very frustrated with the energy and had difficulty distinguishing whether it was positive or negative energy. Simply, when you open yourself to the energy and you sense/hear/feel it approaching you, ask it three times in a row, "Are you coming from the highest vibration?" or "Are you coming from Love and Light?" or "Are you coming with good intentions wanting me to evolve?" Before proceeding, you must sense/hear/feel a definite "Yes" response thrice. To work with beings, you must be capable of sensing energy with all your senses—physically, spiritually, or telepathically. Asking three times and receiving a "YES" answer three times is an assurance that you are communicating with positive energy. If, however, you receive a "NO," or "Wait a minute." or "This is urgent." (or if you sense/ hear/feel nothing), then you are not connecting with the highest positive energy to assist you on your journey. Perhaps some "other" energy wants to confuse you. Do not work with any entity if you do not receive a "Yes" answer. You need to order such energy to go back from where it came. You need to remember that you have free will to do that.

PSYCHIC ATTACK AND PROTECTION WITH GEMSTONES

Anyone can be a victim of a psychic attack anywhere and at any time. If attacked, you may experience sudden energy drain, moodiness, depression, anxiety, panic attack, suicidal thoughts, etc. Recognizing the signs and getting help as soon as possible is crucial. I have been under psychic attacks several times, especially when I started consciously working with energy. Gemstone Therapy (combining gemstone energy) was one of the first energy tools I used to help ward off such attacks. These days, my favorite stone is Moldavite. For those new to energy work, please be wary, as Moldavite's energy may be overwhelming. For a long time, I also favored a combination of black tourmaline and tiger eye for psychic protection. This is a great combination, especially for those learning to work with their energy. Note that each stone offers a little different protection.

Moldavite is an approximately fifteen-million-year-old extraterrestrial stone with amazing high-vibration energy. Its energy will flush your chakras and raise your vibrations, raising your energy upward.

On the other hand, a combination of black tourmaline and tiger eye will create an energy shield around you. This is highly effective for psychic attack protection. I usually recommend this combination to my clients to protect their energy after cleansing. It will also boost courage and may be used as a talisman to overcome deceit and duplicity. In your psychic vision, you can envision these two stones as two fiery warriors of light conjoined in the battle against darkness. Relentlessly, they will shield you against bad vibrations, skillfully deflect possible harm and courageously return negative energy back to its creator. You are protected against negative energy and guarded with powerful, loving light.

I also use black tourmaline and tiger eye to release negative energy from my clients. When I sense a lot of negative energy, especially implants, I place a piece of black tourmaline and tiger eye by each door to seal in the energy and prevent it from finding a hiding place in any part of my house. I call for Archangel Michael, Archangel Azrael, and all of my Light Helpers to escort all negative energy away. These are just basic but effective protective measures.

In the following chapters, you will learn about the different types of negative energy, how to detect it, and how to remove it. You will use this knowledge as Step 2 in the Cleansing Steps (Step 2 varies depending on the specific type of negative energy.)

In chapter 9, you will find the full description of the Cleansing Steps I refer to throughout the book. Please read it all through before you start soul-cleansing energy work.

CHAPTER 5

MECHANICAL IMPLANTS
PARASITES OF NON-HUMAN NATURE

Mechanical Implants are non-human parasites. They are intelligent negative energy. Henceforth, I will refer to them as just implants. Their origin is extraterrestrial - from out of this world, and I repeat myself - not from our planet. They feed off the human body's energy system and can camouflage themselves, becoming transparent and thus being difficult, if not impossible, to detect. Also, victims of alien abductions may have had these implants embedded in their bodies.

You must be experienced in detecting implants, accomplished with practice, to avoid the negative energy fooling you. All implants will directly affect your physical, spiritual, and mental state. Their sole purpose is to confuse, stagnate and control you, preventing you from embracing your unique abilities so that you could fail in your life's mission on Earth.

Viewing implants with your psychic vision will reveal them as weird, mechanic spider-like creatures/devices. What I see are usually oddly shaped forms. They have many legs (or tentacles) with which they root themselves in a person's soul energy, allowing them to control all the energy of the physical body system. The implants attach themselves to the soul first.

Then they gradually descend into the physical body, affecting parts of the major receiving/functioning centers, such as the nervous system, brain, spine, heart, and other vital organs. They attach like invisible leeches and can journey with the soul through its many reincarnations. As aforementioned, they are intelligent. They sabotage spiritual growth and happiness, knowing how to instill physical bodily illnesses, all with the ultimate purpose of providing a distraction from a life's mission. Some function only partly and are activated when a triggering action is taken. Their impact on the human body and its nervous system can be devastating when activated. Many people affected by the implants eventually isolate themselves from the world, refuse help, and begin to demonstrate self-destructive behavior.

Note: The nervous system is always affected by any negative energy.

How do you obtain an implant? The answer is simple and disturbing; you have agreed to it. I have seen this pattern repeating in all the cases I have worked. Something terrible happened somewhere in your Galactic life, and you helped save someone else's life, or in some cases, your own. The scenario is usually that you were in distress or were shown that someone about whom you deeply care was in a life-threatening situation. A so-called good Samaritan appeared and offered to help you. Unfortunately, this good Samaritan was a negative galactic being who did not have the best interest for you—it was a dark being with negative energy, and you knew it. Regrettably, out of despair (but mainly fear of dire circumstances), you accepted the offer anyway, hoping you could eventually eliminate any negative energy from the deal. However, all did not go as planned, and the dark energy stuck with you, for what seemed like an eternity. You accepted this dark entity's deal with your free will (albeit out of fear), but now in your earthly body, you do not consciously remember making the transaction. Now you are simply suffering the consequences.

The good news is that you can re-activate your free will and release the negative energy by acknowledging and accepting what happened. You just have to remember or be reminded. Acknowledgment and conscious acceptance create a mental click in your mind, an essential step toward reestablishing your original blueprint within your body and soul. Denial, anger, sadness, or pity will not help clean this energy out. You would begin the healing process only through conscious knowledge, acceptance, and understanding of what happened. It is a piece of the puzzle that will help to restore your energy system and let you take back your soul energy.

I have been asked, "Where have my guides been? Why didn't they warn me?" and "Why didn't they protect me?" Now, let me ask you what if they had warned you? Would you have listened? Or could you have listened? You have to remember that just as you have free will today, you also had it then. You had a choice. How many times in your current Earth life have you been tricked into something you did not really want to do? Remember that, ultimately, it was your conscious agreement to accept the deal, even if you do not recollect it now.

I wish I could bring comfort with my words, but it does not help much in this case. Instead, consider this a life lesson, but remember that help is available. Therefore, let's move forward. There is a light at the end of the tunnel, and it is time to regain your power!

Note for abductees: If you have been abducted and experimented on by negative extraterrestrial aliens, whether here on Earth or someplace out in the Universe, and if it occurred in your current life or some past lifetime, you may have had an implant placed upon you. Please read the following paragraphs carefully and closely examine the signs described. You will also learn more about them in Chapter 5: Abduction by Negative Extraterrestrial Aliens.

Most Common Signs of Implants
Black Eyes

Almost everyone with an implant confirms having first met people with strange-looking eyes. They encounter complete strangers with unique, piercing, full black glassy eyes (pupils). They claim that they sensed negative and evil energy coming from these strangers. They say these strangers acted unpredictably, making them feel deeply uncomfortable, scared, intimidated, and confused. They did not know if these strangers were terrible or evil. They also state that these strangers behaved strangely and seemed upset or angry easily for no reason. There is a reason for this, which I will explain in the next section: hostile behavior. It is helpful to realize that the situation with strangers with black eyes is not what it appears. Their eyes and aggressive behavior merely reflect the vibration/energy that the implant inside is exerting from within you.

The key is understanding that the eyes are the windows to the soul. Soul energy shines through your eyes and will touch someone else's soul while making contact—a conscious soul connection eye-to-eye. I want you to stop briefly and notice a difference between sensing someone's soul through clairsentience (feeling the energy) and direct eye contact. Initially, I thought implants only emanated negative energy through one's physical being, controlling one's chi-life force. Then my guides helped me understand that implants are powerful, intelligent, and vicious.

One day, I received a simple answer when I was asking the Lights of the Universe to help me recognize when implants are present. I was reminded of the common denominator in almost all cases: the strangers' strange black eyes.

Example: I worked with Sally for some time. She was a beautiful lady in her early fifties. Her non-human parasite was in her heart, her soul. As I psychically read her past lives, I was led to her galactic life in a different world. My visions are usually full of vivid colors, but unfortunately, this one was only black and white. I could see her as a child, maybe around eight years old. She was driving with her family in a vehicle (or what we can describe as a vehicle). I was seeing everything through her eyes. Looking out the window, I noticed unusual buildings and trees. Then, I saw her home. She looked at her mother, who sat in the front seat, and I could feel how much Sally loved her. Sally was also very aware of her unique abilities and special energy. Suddenly, she saw a metallic spider climbing on her mother's shoulder. She immediately knew this spider was a soul-controlling device and that it would kill her mother, who was full of love energy. Sally knew the spider wanted to control and drain all the energy from her mother and that her mother would ultimately die. In her mind, she silently agreed to take her mother's place and host this spider/implant to save her mother's life. Since Sally had unique energy, she could sacrifice herself and survive.

In this lifetime, however, it became difficult for Sally to make new friends. Whenever she would make a female friend and feel happy, something went wrong, and the relationship ended. For most of her life, Sally felt lonely and isolated. Finally, she found the work she loved amongst other females and made many friends. However, her happiness lasted only a short time. Out of the blue, she became ill with an environmental illness and had to stop working. That led to isolation once again. She also said she had met many people with strange-looking black eyes who exhibited odd, aggressive, and angry behavior toward her for no apparent reason. She was carrying the implant in her current life, and it was controlling her. The behavior and the black eyes she encountered with these strangers were merely the subconscious responses to her implant's vibration/energy. She saw the reflection of her implant in the strangers' eyes and hostile behavior. These experiences made her feel depressed, sad, lonely, rejected, and isolated, precisely what the implant wanted her to feel so it could keep harnessing her energy.

Hostile Behavior

Another sign that people have implants is that they usually attract other strangers who seem to exhibit hostile behavior. It is interesting to note that not the strangers are the problem, but rather the implant's energy from within the victim that literally makes "strangers" act hostile. As I described previously, when a victim of an implant meets complete strangers with strange-looking black eyes, the strangers become angry, mad, violent, aggressive, etc., toward the victim for no particular reason. The victim doesn't understand the strangers' odd behavior. Often, these strangers are not evil beings at all, or even "possessed" as they may appear. Most likely, they are not even consciously aware of their odd behavior. What the victim sees is the reflection of the dark implant that is in control. I want to point out that this is the victim's subconscious mind receiving triggering vibrations from the implant. It intends to exert negative energy through the victim's eye onto the strangers' eyes through regular eye contact. The implant wants to repel all other souls near its victim to prevent and block its victim from getting too close to anyone or possibly getting help.

Example: I worked with Tina for over a year before we could detect and remove her implant. Tina was a gorgeous lady in her early forties, but whenever she went out or wanted to meet people, she received strange and uncomfortable reactions from unknown men and women. Most of the time, she remembered that these people had strange black eyes. She was puzzled. Tina was highly accomplished, well-spoken, traveled, intelligent, and self-confident. It did not make any sense. At one of the sessions (we had distance sessions), Tina shared with me that she wore nonprescription glasses as a fashion accent to her glamorous image. Intuitively, she figured out that when she wore the glasses, people reacted differently to her. I didn't quite understand. I speculated she would feel confident wearing the glasses, while not wearing them would make her lack confidence. Perhaps she was projecting this energy on others subconsciously. However, Tina disagreed with my observation. She said she felt the same about herself whether she wore the glasses or not. I believed her. She added that with the glasses, she felt protected, so she wore them often. I was left puzzled.

A few months later, I went to the planetarium for a family outing and saw a demonstration of how different light rays can travel through or are blocked with various objects (including glass). Then it hit me, and my guides responded, "Oh, you finally are getting it!" Her nonprescription glasses blocked the implant from projecting its negative energy or vibration onto others through her eyes. The glasses were blinding the non-human parasite so that it could not make eye contact with people who the victim encountered. I was so thrilled to learn this!

Note: It is expected that when psychic healers assist someone who unknowingly has an implant, they will be unable to detect this hidden negative energy immediately because the implant is transparent/invisible. This energy also tricks the healer into believing that the victim's future looks bright and hopeful. Since it is intelligent energy, it also knows how to distinguish when the victim is dealing with someone who is not "seeing it" and, therefore, does not pose any threat versus someone who can play an essential and integral role in the victim's life. When the implant feels threatened, it will do all it can to repel anyone it feels will jeopardize its continued hold on the victim's soul. Remember that implants are intelligent and vicious. They are a dark matter life force.

Black and White

Another common sign is black-and-white energy in a victim's energy field. When you first read the energy of someone who has an implant, the energy may feel very good. The aura may appear excellent and healthy, with the body's energy also appearing to be healthy, even if the victim has expressed other signs of seeing people with back eyes and the feeling of repelling others. Please remember that negative energy is clever and can camouflage well!

When you suspect someone has a non-human parasite, you must read/scan the energy in the past time. I like to go 5 minutes back (in my mind) and read the energy in the past. The difference in energy reports from scanning the body in the current and past times will give you a clue about what you are dealing with. The difference could be astonishing! The first red flag should arise when you cannot see or sense the full colors of the aura or chakras. If they appear light, blurry, or only in black and white, there is a problem. This is especially true when you read the energy from past lives because negative energy wants to confuse you and discourage you. You may literary feel like the color has been removed from the victim's soul. The implant is working on slowly sucking away the victim's life essence.

At this moment, you may even question your abilities to sense/see subtle energy colors during the reading, but you should not get discouraged and stay focused. The implant will do all it can to confuse you!

The inability to see/sense in full color and only see/feel in black and white, even if it is just for a moment, signalizes that something is wrong. The physical body should constantly be vibrating with and resonating in many vivid colors, both horizontally and vertically.

Note: If an implant is in the body, it will appear dark and feel like a bump. On the other hand, an illness will appear as a dark mass. You should be clear if you locate the dark mass with some colors in some parts. This is likely an illness, not a mechanical parasite, and your client may need medical assistance and different approaches to healing. For example, cancer appears as a big black blob, but it also feels like a black hole sucking in energy when you put your hand over the affected area.

Feeling of Discontent – Feeling that Something is Wrong

Not all people with depression are victims of a non-human parasite. When diagnosing yourself or working with your client, you would need to thoroughly research your or your client's past to arrive at reasons for depression, sadness, loneliness, rejection, or isolation.

Any or all the feelings mentioned above originate from unfounded fear. You have to name and face all the fears to get to the bottom of the problem (you are finding the root of the problem). The implants will create fears that appear natural and genuine even though they are not to try and fool you and your client. Interestingly, people with non-human parasites are very old, gifted souls, and the implants do all they can to hold them back and keep them from fully embracing their unique abilities. It is vital that before you start cleansing, you acknowledge that non-human parasites are intelligent, controlling, albeit evil, potent devices.

Note: When one has depression caused by an implant, the nervous system is severely damaged and will need extensive healing. Depression is not healed by simply removing the implant. It is a complicated condition, and you will need counseling, light energy work, and help to set a new energy pattern that will take up to several weeks or maybe even months to complete.

Postponing Help

If you realize you could have an implant or once you diagnose someone with a non-human implant, you will be faced with the real challenge. In both cases, you may, and often will, feel very drained, busy, or discouraged before the session begins. It may start a few days beforehand. I recommend that you take care of yourself at this critical time!

Your client (inflicted with the implant) will also recollect many of his/her current life experiences before the session, making him/her feel even more depressed and most likely want to postpone the session. Many of my clients have confided in me that they wanted to cancel our sessions because they had felt physical ailments such as heart palpitations, lightheadedness, and nausea, making them fear what would happen in our sessions.

You and your client will feel like that because the implant knows what will happen and will try to stop the upcoming cleansing process at all costs. It will try to block you both as much as possible, and physical torment and fear only amplify its energy. I cannot tell you how often my clients have canceled a much-needed cleansing before the session. I recommend that you, as the healer, schedule a date/time for a session and stick with it, no matter what. I always tell my clients that no matter how badly they feel or are scared, they just need to make it to my house for the session.

If you are doing the cleansing yourself with no other help, it is helpful to have all the steps you will follow written down in some notes that you can use. Trust me, you will be thankful for that.

REMOVING IMPLANTS – PARASITES OF NON-HUMAN NATURE

Cleansing Steps (CS)
Step 1 - Preparation
Step 2 - Removing Implants
Step 3 - Chakra Healing
Step 4 - Activation of Self-Healing Green Color Energy
Step 5 - Activation of Spinning Points
Step 6 - Activation of the Universal Light

Before removing the implant, begin with initial step 1 of CS found in chapter 9.

STEP 2 – REMOVING IMPLANTS

Summary: A body may visually appear healthy, even with an implant. The implant is negative intelligent energy and will hide in the present, showing a false present or future. The best way to detect the implant is by scanning and reading the energy of the client in the past time. The energy with an implant will be black and white and lack any other colors. On the other hand, the energy of an illness within the body may resemble a black mass. Still, the outer surrounding area and other body parts will retain their vivid natural colors. This practice teaches you to distinguish between implants and illness energy.

READING ENERGY IN THE PAST TIME

Begin by raising your vibrations. (as described in chapter 3)

First, you will read your client's energy in the present time. If you do distant healing, follow the same instructions. Do it quick and avoid getting tricked into doing any healing or cleansing at this time. You will have enough time soon enough.

Start with the root chakra and continue upward. Position yourself at your client's feet. Pass your hands slowly over his/her entire body and locate the outline of his/her aura. Then, take mental notes, and say aloud (if you want), what needs to be healed and/or adjusted, but wait to analyze or make any plans!

Now, scan your client's energy again, this time in the past. Once again, start by your client's feet (and work upward), set your intention, and/or state aloud, "I am scanning 5 minutes in the past." Then, pretend that you are jumping into the past. All it takes is to mentally focus and tell yourself you are seeing 5 minutes prior. It is that simple!

Then, once again, take mental notes, and say aloud (if you want) what needs to be healed and/or adjusted. Notice if there is any difference in the chakra colors you have seen prior, any new "bumps" in the energy (an implant could feel like a bump that has not been there before), or anything different, but do not analyze or make any plans yet!

Examples of implants scanning 5 minutes in the past:

Sally is an Arcturian starseed healer with an implant on her soul/heart, preventing her from soul growth.

Michael is a Lyran/Pleiadian Starseed with an implant behind his ear, preventing him from hearing messages.

Mary is a Sirian starseed with three egg-shaped implants on the back side of her brain, blocking the pineal gland and preventing her from receiving any knowledge.

Lora is an Andromedan/Sirian starseed with several implants, the most prevalent one on her throat, preventing her from speaking freely or communicating with others.

John is an Andromedan/Pleiadian starseed with an implant close to his wrist, causing heart problems.

Many times, an implant will twine itself into the body's spine. In your psychic vision, it may appear like an eel or serpent (this is very different than the kundalini serpent.). Commonly, implants control the body's nervous system. That is why the nervous system needs to be healed after removal. This may take several sessions.

DETECTING AND NEUTRALIZING AN IMPLANT

Now you will compare the two scans. If there is a difference between the scan in the present time and the scan in the past, then you are dealing with an implant.

Remember, for the next step, you will still be working in the past time!

After comparing, go back to the past time energy, and as soon as you detect the implant, place both of your hands, palms facing down, on the area and surround it with Love and Light energy. The energy will come through your soul. Your soul energy could be your choice, either white or gold in color. But you can also use a color that strongly vibrates with your star (home world) if your guides suggest it. Imagine enclosing the implant in the shell of that energy. Remember, you are still working in the past time. Now neutralize/freeze this enclosed implant by setting the intention to neutralize/freeze. (This is only temporary.) Now you can ask your guides to help you to see how it got there, where it originated, and its purpose.

MAKE A CONSCIOUS CONNECTION – CREATE A MENTAL CLICK

Inform your client about what is going on and what has occurred. Share details about what you have experienced so far— seeing/sensing/feeling—along with any information provided to you by your guides. Then ask if she/he remembers the original details of agreeing to have this implant. This is a very critical moment because there should be some similarity between your client's past life (lives) and the current one. Usually, negative feelings, such as loneliness, sadness, unhappiness, and fear (especially fear because it belongs to the implant), are the most common emotions that continue and stay with the soul. Therefore, it is essential to discover the core of any specific fear and determine how this "fear-based" implant took control.

You will need to help your client accept what has happened. This will allow for a conscious click to occur inside him/her. In the same way, your client consciously agreed to be the host for this negative energy, now s/he must also consciously decide to let it go. Why not just get rid of it? The reason is that if you do not consciously acknowledge the reality of the situation and intentionally ask for help in removing it, it will most likely find its way back.

REMOVING THE IMPLANT

Place both of your hands, palms facing down, on the area. Raise your vibration again, and increase it as high as possible, letting your soul light shine into the implant. Next, focus on your soul light, feel the vibration of the love frequency, and feel it pulsating through the essence of your whole being. Feel immense love for everyone and everything, even the implant. Ask your guides, your soul family, to assist you with removing this negative energy. (Your guides will escort the implant to its home. Every energy, good or bad, belongs somewhere.) But your guides need your help to begin the process. You will literally burn this energy out with your soul light and love. (You are creating an immense light burst, similar to a nuclear blast.) Then, while you are sending the light, send love vibrations along with it. If any chants come to mind, say them aloud. I speak the Language of Light and use ritual chants in my cleansings. However, the Language of Light is unnecessary to successfully remove the implant. If any chants come to you, just say them. If not, it is fine. You can also bless this implant with divine energy, say a prayer, or do anything with a positive attitude infused with love and light. You will be surprised how fast the implant will go!

Keep sending your powerful light and unconditional love toward the implant. The implant will not be able to bear it, and your client may feel significant pain and/or discomfort, but it should be temporary and not last more than a few minutes. This may be intense but hold your high-energy vibration as long as possible. Once the implant has been removed, you will notice a significant decrease in the energy flow and will also experience a sense of relief in both you and your client. Take a deep breath and let it all out, feeling calm and content. There is no time limit on how long this process should take. Just use your intuition and project your soul's energy until you sense that you have achieved your healing purpose.

After removing the implant, continue with CS's remaining steps 3, 4, 5, and 6.

After the Removal

After removal, the mind, body, and spirit must fully heal, and follow-up sessions are required!

Two or three follow-up sessions will be necessary. These sessions, once a week, will focus on energy work for your client. You will need to revitalize the nervous system and energize the chakras. Ensure that "color" is back and that it vibrates in purity. Spiritual counseling or working with a life coach or advisor is highly recommended to set new goals for your client and assist him/her on a new path. Remember, your client must learn to live without something implanted for what seemed like an eternity!

You may think removing the non-human parasite was the hardest part of the process, but the real challenge is still ahead of you.

Now that you have removed the intelligent negative energy, it is time to fill the void. Please realize that this energy was with you or your client's soul for perhaps millions of years, and it will not be easy to learn to live without it. It is similar to amputating a limb for survival. The person may be thankful and optimistic to be alive, although at the cost of a limb. However, the weariness of life can take over, and depression may follow. People who have had implants removed usually feel excellent for several days after the removal. However, depending on how extensive the energy damage was, they will experience "withdrawal" (like from drug addiction) and hit a deep low within a few weeks. It is almost like their bodies finally realize what has happened and, crazy as it sounds, crave that negative energy. Their bodies and souls grew to be dependent on it. Now new rules need to be set and followed. It is necessary that new energy habits also be embraced. This can be compared to people who quit smoking, drinking, using drugs, etc. The best advice you can follow after removing the implant is, "Stay positive! Change the way you think; change the way you live!"

Even though it will be difficult for you or your client to live without the implant initially, there is help. I highly recommend that you learn and teach the basic level of self-energy healing and urge to use it several times a week, if not daily! Each person with whom I have worked that has had an implant has also unknowingly had the fantastic ability for healing and being psychic. Implants prey on people with hidden abilities to avoid letting them become aware of such skills. Many of these people eventually give up on their abilities due to not being able to find the right kind of help, at the right time, because of the implants. There is a reason why you are reading this book. You are a Warrior of Light and have all it takes to assist your brothers and sisters!

"Knowledge is a seed of light. From knowledge, wisdom is born. The power that arises from wisdom is limitless. Thus, the limitations and lack of knowledge are only in our mind!"

TOOLS FOR SELF-HELP

You can help yourself to ward off implants. Try using Moldavite. It is an approximately fifteen-million-year-old extraterrestrial stone with unique energies that protect against a hostile environment. Its energy will flush your chakras. It will also assist you in raising your vibration. When you are on a higher vibration, you can expel and repel any implant within you.

Real Moldavite is tektite natural glass. If the regular glass can blind the non-human parasite, as mentioned before, then Moldavite may be the stone you need if you are dealing with an implant. It can confuse it and create a high vibrational environment within your body that will become hostile to it.

Note: I recommend having a piece of Moldavite while working on cleansing an implant. You can have it as a piece of jewelry, ornament, or a small, tumbled piece in your pocket. Other great gemstones for protection are black tourmaline and tiger eye. You may also want to research orgonite and its use for energy protection. I personally have orgonite devices in my house and love their energy. Many other crystals have protective energy; these are just some of my favorites.

Consider teaching others about protecting personal energy by opening and closing it and raising your vibration. Educate your clients on the first level of energy healing techniques to locate their chakras and reenergize energy as needed.

CHAPTER 6

ABDUCTION BY
NEGATIVE EXTRATERRESTRIALS

What does it mean to have been abducted by extraterrestrials? It means being victimized, taken against one's free will, experimented on, and perhaps making significant life choices based on fear against your healthy judgment. So far, all of the abductees with whom I have worked have been tricked into accepting mechanical implants. These mechanical implants are non-human parasites and are intelligent negative energy. Henceforth, I will refer to them as just implants. Again, implants can only inhabit someone's body with permission, under free will. However, when tortured, anyone will most likely agree to anything, albeit under duress, to survive.

It is challenging to work with an abductee who has been forced to undergo painful physical experiments by malevolent extraterrestrials. Please know this requires a lot of patience from the abductee and the healer. There is extensive emotional damage to the abductee's psyche, especially if he/she can consciously remember the painful details of the ordeal. The abductee's nervous system is also severely damaged. The recovery period will be slow, taking time, patience, and dedication to restore the original energy grid. Several sessions will be needed, so they should be scheduled accordingly. Also, the abductee must learn to raise the soul's vibration and the basic form of energy work and apply it as often as needed.

Everything you have read and learned about implants, including the telltale signs, also applies to abduction. The difference between abductees and victims being controlled by implants is that abductees have been given the implant in this lifetime. In contrast, victims who are being controlled by implants were given the implant eons ago. Also, abductees will more likely have a partial or complete memory of the abduction while in a subconscious state of shock. While working with abductees, pay close attention to restoring the abductee's psyche, nervous system, and energy grid, and continue doing energy work for as long as is needed. It may take several months until new light energy has settled and the body is used to it. A new pattern also needs to be set! The fear that another abduction will take place must be confronted and dispelled. Teach and provide the abductee with self-protection tools so that s/he is no longer afraid. Raising energy vibrations is the simplest yet effective tool.

It is easier to remove mechanical implants someone had for gazillion years than to help abductees restore their energy and faith in this world.

When working with a client and establishing that she/he has been abducted, you may be visited by Grey Aliens (commonly known as "Greys"). Most abductions have been done by Grey Aliens, as they have been "enslaved" by the Dark Side. In recent years, Greys have been allowed to rise into the higher vibration, evolve, and leave the Dark side. It is essential to understand that they were created by the Dark side and raised, programmed, and reinforced to do this job. At this time, not all Greys want to change their "lifestyle" and join the ascension process, although some are embracing the opportunity. Through my work experience, I concluded that Greys need to work off their karma before they can evolve - the same as humans. They must prove they mean good and are committed to walking harmoniously with other benevolent star nations.

Now, how do Greys prove themselves? When you work with a client who has been abducted by Greys, a Grey may visit you. If this occurs, you want to test Grey's energy. Is it coming with the best of intentions for you and your client? Does he answer "Yes" three times to your question? If he responds with a "yes" three times, he wants to help you undo what has been done to your client. It may sound odd, but if the Grey comes to you to assist you in releasing the implant and healing the trauma, then it is accepting full responsibility for what has been done (by his kind) to your client. This will have a tremendous positive impact on Grey's karma, even their collective consciousness karma. This will allow Grey (not the others, unless they also come to you) to move toward God's Source (light). While assisting you, it will advise you what happened, where the implant is located, or how to remove it. It will provide you with crucial details that will help heal your client!

This allows Greys to prove to the Council of Light that they accepted themself to be worthy and chose to be benevolent beings, part of the intergalactic star community. Again, usually, you will work individually with a Grey, not with a group of Greys. It is essential to realize that only some of them are ready to be responsible for their actions, and they want to change. The ones that do change know that helping an abductee will put them, temporarily, on the Dark Side's Most Wanted list, as they will betray their Dark kind. You do not need to worry about that, as it is between the Council of Light and the Council of Dark. You may be surprised how well they work together to resolve what may appear as conflict. No one should ever live in fear and under control. Everyone has the right to free will and perform good deeds.

In my experience, when a Grey comes to you, while you do this kind of work, it wants to establish a working relationship. It is totally up to you whether you accept its help. The Grey may need to work with you until it has proven itself to the Council of Light.

Never in my work experience have I had a Grey directly assist me in hands-on healing or removing an implant. It generally provides me with mental assistance, giving me important information, such as the location of the implant and the damage that the implant is expected to cause. Then, it may give me specific details about the abduction itself. It is important to share information directly with my client. It helps the client understand that s/he was a victim and not at fault. The Grey may also provide input on healing your client's nervous system, which most likely suffered extensive damage. The Grey is working his way up toward enlightenment. Also, working together will not put you in a situation of being "attacked" by other Greys. This is why it communicates with you telepathically rather than with verbal speech. However, I recommend practicing invisibility to negative energy for the removal procedure.

In summary, the benevolent Grey who wants to work off its negative karma (heal his soul) will want to establish direct communication with you. It is your choice to accept or reject it. If you accept it, the Grey may also guide others who need help toward you until permission is granted to "cross over to the light."

Remember: The Grey does not join in giving healing energy or any energy work. It merely provides you with information and directions, nothing more.

Note: If you are an abductee and healing yourself, I recommend finding a trusted friend for assistance. Read this book together and ask for clear, non-judgmental feedback on how you are progressing in healing and becoming yourself. When you set your mind that you can do this yourself and want to heal your soul from all the traumas that have happened to you, you can do this. You are on your way and have all you need to do this!

Removing Implants from Abduction

Cleansing Steps (CS)
Step 1 - Preparation
Step 2 - Removing Implants from Abduction
Step 3 - Chakra Healing
Step 4 - Activation of Self-Healing Green Color Energy
Step 5 - Activation of Spinning Points
Step 6 - Activation of the Universal Light

Before removing the implant, begin with initial step 1 of CS found in chapter 9

Step 2 – Removing Implants from Abduction
When working with someone who has been abducted and experimented on by negative ETs, you do not want to attract that energy toward yourself and your family. For this reason, you will practice "invisibility." As with mechanical implants, before the session, you and your client may feel confused and/or distracted. You should write the steps down to stick with them. Stay focused!

Becoming Invisible to negative Energy
Separate your energy cords completely from your client. Use your intention. You can state in your mind or out loud, "I ask to separate my energy cords and all energy links from my client/friend."

Imagine yourself in a golden shell of energy.

Raise your soul vibrations. Imagine a bright light bulb inside your chest, in your heart chakra (where your soul sits). Imagine your heart chakra gradually growing bigger and bigger until this light illuminates your whole being and shines way beyond your body.

Once again, focus on your soul energy in your heart chakra. Imagine going inward without diminishing your soul light.

Slow down all your energy through deep, slow breaths.

Tell yourself to be in your galactic form: "I am changing in my galactic form." You will sense your energy rise rapidly, and you may feel an increase in your size.

You will feel the energy rise. You may see yourself in your original skin. You may feel bigger or smaller depending on your galactic origin :) With this energy, you will start your energy work.

Proceed with your work - each case is different. If you are working with benevolent Grey, utilize the knowledge given to you. If you sense an implant or controlling device, follow the implant removal process from previous chapter 4.

- Reading energy in the past time.

-Detecting and neutralizing an implant.

- Make a conscious connection - create a mental "click."

- Removing the implant.

When you are done, remove all energy links and imprints (disconnect your energy links from your client.

Even though you were disconnected initially, your energy will connect while you are doing energy work.) Treat the traumatized soul by filling it with love and light energy.

When you are done with Step 2, do not forget to come back into your body through your heart chakra and ground yourself.

Note: Do not let your ego convince you that you are "invincible."

After you are finished, continue with the remaining steps 3, 4, 5, and 6 of CS.

AFTER REMOVAL

As with those affected by the mechanical implant, removing negative energy is the first step. The true challenge comes after. Explaining to your client that more than one session is needed is essential.

Arrange various sessions and tailor them as needed. Some people will insist that the implant is still there; this is not true. They may feel it is there because their body is not yet accustomed to new energy. Work with your client at least once or twice a week. Talk about it; go back in the past and assist the soul in healing from trauma. The physical nervous system will be hugely affected and need many healings. Work with energizing the spine, chakras, and whole nervous system. Internal organs - small intestines, bladder, and kidney are often affected, as they are the main energy pathways for the nervous system. They need to reenergize and devote some energy to healing these organs.

Many sessions are needed—life coaching, support groups, refocusing of thinking, setting goals, and learning energy healing are reasonable steps in recovery.

Every time after the follow-up session, complete the healing steps 3,4,5, and 6 described later in this book. There will be many, many layers to go through and heal. Before you take on this job, explain to your client that s/he needs to meet you halfway and be willing to heal, acknowledge and accept what happened. She/he will no longer be a victim and need help reclaiming the lost power. Help the client realize that identifying as a "victim" is precisely what this energy wants. Also, know that you will be exhausted after sessions like this, so take the rest of the day off or take it easy. Only work with another client once you completely cleanse yourself.

Lights of the Universe do not recommend using hypnosis techniques as a healing remedy for those who have been abducted. You may learn what happened from hypnosis, but the body is physically affected. If healing comes from a "conscious place" into a "conscious memory," it has a better, faster, more lasting effect. Remember, your client has to work as hard as you do to change his life and be free.

If you are using this book for healing yourself, write in a journal, mark your progress, and stay focused. Do not get distracted by the energy. Seek help from a trusted healer if you feel the need.

GREY LOOM

While working on this book, I also worked with a gifted artist Ashley Ruiz, who can see beings through her mind's eye, and we met many beings of light. One of them was a Grey alien who called himself Loom.

If you are drawn to work with Greys, consider starting with Loom. Following is Loom's channeled message and direction on how to work with him.

Loom: "Fear may paralyze your ability to thrive. You can change this!"

Message: We were created to thrive on human fears. Our main task was, and for some still is, to connect to your emotional and nervous system and press the "fear" buttons within you, making you paranoid, anxious, afraid, and ultimately emotionally paralyzed and unable to fulfill your "light path" destiny. Like you, many of us have evolved and found Light, Love, and unity with oneness. I now walk on the path of light and offer you my guidance and knowledge. I can assist you to see and understand if you, or someone else, have been harmed or controlled by Greys. I can guide you in removing any implants that may influence you and start your blueprint-restoring process. I will assist you, but as the Council of Light requested, I may not join your energy work.

Light Initiation: Say out loud or in your mind, "I ask and thank you for being connected with the Grey light being Loom." Then ask the following question three times: "Is this Grey light being Loom?" You MUST sense/hear/feel the "yes" answer three times before proceeding. To work with Loom, you must be capable of sensing energy in your body, hearing with your physical or spiritual ears, and obtaining telepathically or using automatic writing to receive an answer. Ask three times, and three times you must receive the YES response. If you receive "no" or "wait a minute" or "this is urgent" or you hear/sense nothing—if you are not receiving a YES answer three times, then you are not connecting with Loom. Perhaps some "other" energy wants to confuse you. Do not work with Loom or any entity if you cannot make a "yes" connection and order the energy to return where it came from.

Note: IMPORTANT!!! When working with them, you must learn to test energy and beings, especially Greys. Please know that some of you will feel repelled by this energy, which means it is not for you to work with. Some will feel intrigued or drawn to Loom's energy.

CHAPTER 7

EARTHBOUND SPIRITS

SPIRIT ATTACHMENTS THAT HAVE NOT CROSSED TO THE OTHER SIDE

A spirit attachment is the earthbound spirit of a deceased person who (for various reasons) refuses to cross over to the other side. One of these reasons may be confusion: not being in the physical body and not yet in the light of the other side, a state often referred to as the in-between stage. While in this in-between stage, some earthbound spirits look for a physical vessel to attach themselves to remain connected to the physical world, the only world they know at this point in time.

The attached spirit may be a family member, friend, acquaintance, or stranger. When you are spiritually open, your inner light is like a beacon, a lighthouse in the darkness of these spirits. Naturally, your light will attract them, and you will become their hope to return home, whether you like it or not.

You can easily pick up an earthbound spirit in hospitals, hospice centers, cemeteries, antique shops, shows, haunted places (usually where something tragic occurred), places where people committed suicide, war/battlefields and monuments, etc. The time frame does not matter in the spirit world. I once met a spirit contemplating vengeance on those who had killed him over 200 years before.

How Does It Feel To Have A Spirit Attached To You?

You may feel sad, angry, depressed, or confused for no apparent reason. This feeling often appears suddenly and has nothing to do with your life. You may have a great family and a successful job, and suddenly you will feel like you are becoming someone else, as if someone else is taking over your life. Your personality, the food you crave, or your interests may change. You may experience nightmares. You may dream of your loved ones who have passed away or of others you may not even know. You may see them decaying in the dream; you may see them sad and crying or exhibiting other unsettling behavior, behavior so intense and shocking that you may feel you are trapped in the middle of a horror movie.

Here are a few examples: When I first started consciously communicating with spirits, some thought using my body to feel human again would be funny. I consciously allowed this. One night my ex-husband was putting a wet finishing coat on our wooden kitchen floor. It took him some considerable time, and he asked me not to walk on the floor for a few hours. I agreed and watched a TV show. Then out of nowhere, I stood up and walked into the kitchen. After walking back and forth on the wet floor, I stopped suddenly and, seeing the damage I had just done, wondered, "What have I just done?" I could not, however, remember walking there. I thought I was just thinking about something else and forgot about the state of the kitchen floor, so I let it go. Of course, my ex was very upset, but he fixed the problem. Strangely enough, I was not feeling that bad about it at all. Then, believe it or not, I did it again once he finished the repairs! At this point, he became livid and yelled unkind words at me. Who could blame him?

Yet again, I did not feel guilty. I remained calm and did not understand why I had walked on that floor. Calmly, I went to bed for the night. In that state where one is half awake and half asleep, it hit me. I was not behaving like myself. Why was I not upset at the damage I had done to the floor? Twice? Why was I not upset at my ex's yelling at me, which was atypical behavior. I realized I was not behaving as usual when the sudden knowing hit me. I had a spirit attachment and a nasty one! That was when I began my quest to learn all I could about spirit attachments and psychic protection.

Two other memorable events occurred when I moved to Chicago. I was working with a veteran who came from Iraq. His friends were killed in action, and he suffered from survivor's guilt. When we connected, the spirits of his army friends filled the room, giving him specific details to confirm their real presence there. The session went well. Afterward, I noticed that one soldier liked to hang around after the others had gone. I did not mind. I did not know much about Chicago yet, and I loved to take long walks to think and relax. One day when I went for a walk, I noticed the soldier was there just behind me. Later when I told my husband about my joyful walk, his eyes popped out, and he told me that I had walked through a dangerous neighborhood! Upon hearing that, I realized why the soldier was walking with me.

On another occasion, the same soldier spirit accompanied me to a park swimming pool, and I suddenly noticed myself checking out the females and having thoughts about them. I knew these were not my thoughts. I enjoyed our connection, but it was time for the soldier to go. When the spirit starts changing your personality, it is time to say goodbye. Since then, I have not consciously allowed spirits to attach to me.

My client Chloe experienced a spirit attachment. Chloe came to me with many problems connected to her nervous system that had, she reported, forced her (long before we met) to leave an outstanding job that she loved. In a healing session with Chloe, I sensed that a spirit attachment was involved in her problems. The spirit attachment was her brother, and she confirmed that her twin brother had passed away in a motorcycle accident ten years before. They had an extremely close bond. His passing was unexpected and a shock to him and his family. Instead of crossing to the other side, he wanted to spend more time with his sister. He loved her so much. At first, it was easy to be with her, but because he did not cross to the other side, his energy became heavier, and he needed to attach himself more to her.

During one of our sessions, I guided Chloe back to her old memories. She could see when she started changing; she was becoming more like her brother after his passing. Her preferences in food, lifestyle, and personality had all changed. This behavior continued for the next ten years. When I worked with Chloe and identified the presence of her brother, I also sensed that her brother felt guilty for remaining attached to Chloe and having an undue influence on her life, but he was also filled with fear of crossing to the other side. He understood how he had been altering Chloe's life, not necessarily for her benefit. I asked him why he was so afraid to seek the light. I could sense that he was a very good person during his lifetime. Why was he so scared to walk into the light? I was astounded by his answer.

Chloe and Jake (her brother) had parents with strong religious beliefs: Even one sin would condemn one to hell. The children were taught that God was vengeful. Because Jake understood how he negatively changed his sister's life, he believed he had committed a terrible sin by not crossing over and attaching himself to his sister. He thought he would go to hell for it, as preached by his parents and the church they attended. Chloe confirmed that they were raised with these beliefs. It took considerable time to convince Jake that there was no hell. (There are different places for complicated souls, but there is a better time to discuss that, as this was not the case here.) He was so scared and believed that if, for example, you stole one candy, you would end up in hell with no redemption at all. How tragic. The good news is that Jake could cross to the other side and is now in Heaven.

Sometimes a soul who leaves the body does not realize that s/he can return from the other side and become a guardian angel soon after physical passing and get trapped in between. To avoid this, you can raise your spiritual awareness in your current lifetime, and this knowledge will stay with you when you pass away. Once you reach this level of awareness all knowledge gained from this life will remain with you (after passing), and you will have a much easier time crossing since you will understand the process and be aware of what is happening.

Another example of spirit attachment concerned a married couple that moved into a new apartment. Soon after moving in, Marie started to feel odd sensations and uncomfortable feelings, as if the place was haunted. She thought it was just her imagination playing tricks on her. Things moved spontaneously, and the couple was unsure what was happening. They lived in that apartment for about a year and knew there was "something" in there. Things became scary when Marie started to see shadows and dark faces. They ran scared out of the apartment and thought that if they moved away, the dark spirits would not follow them. Spending a night in Marie's mother's house sounded like a good idea, but to their dismay, they had nightmares and heard the dark spirits talking to them.

The couple started questioning the apartment manager to learn whether the apartment's history was causing the problems they were experiencing. They discovered the tenants who had lived in the apartment before had committed suicide. The landlord did not want to share that story when renting the apartment. Since the previous couple committed suicide, their souls were trapped. All they could do was bother the new occupants hoping they would help the suicide couple cross over. The couple did not know that when a soul is stuck in-between, it may do anything to get your attention because you are a possible light to Heaven. Once all this was revealed, we could peacefully assist the trapped souls crossing into the light.

How Does Soul Become Earthbound?

When you are close to passing, usually about three to seven days (give or take), angels and family members are sent to assist you in crossing to the other side. Often, we hear stories of people in their final days talking about family members visiting and conversing with them. The other side works hard to prepare souls for smooth passing. While visitations from the other side are very comforting, ultimately, it is our free will to choose to cross to the other side. There may be various reasons why the soul feels it cannot leave a particular place. Perhaps the soul needs more time to complete some unfinished business, to say goodbye, or is in denial in accepting its own death.

Unfortunately, not crossing over is a mistake, and instead of gaining a little extra time, the soul becomes an earthbound spirit, becoming lost and experiencing heavy energy. At this stage, the spirit can see what is happening but cannot interact with the physical plane. The spirit has to cross to the other side to become light and connect with universal consciousness.

ACCIDENTAL DEATH

Passing away in an accident may shock the soul. When a sudden unexpected death occurs, the soul is torn from its earthly vessel (physical body), possibly becoming perplexed. One second, you are well and alive, having plans for the future; the next, you are hovering above your body and wondering what happened.

Please know that angels, family spirits, and beings of light are ALWAYS there to assist the soul in crossing. Thus, when a soul refuses to cross over, it could be in shock, experiencing denial, or enraged over its sudden death. Assistance is offered for some time, but if the soul is stubborn, the window of opportunity closes temporarily, and the soul becomes an earthbound spirit. Once more, notice that everything is happening based on free will. The soul cannot be forced, ordered, or induced to cross to the other side. It has to cross over of its own free will.

SUICIDE

Suicide is the desperate act of a soul wanting to get out of its physical body. Some people think committing suicide will solve all their problems. Unfortunately, no matter how difficult and overwhelming life may be, ending your life is not a solution. When I work with spirits who commit suicide, they are usually confused. The typical scenario is that instead of being relieved of the burden of life, the soul is trapped "in-between" energy fields and keeps reliving over and over the moments of its own suicide and the last days leading toward the suicide. I know this may be difficult to hear for those whose loved ones have committed suicide. Very few souls who commit suicide can cross over to the other side immediately; it depends on the level of soul growth. Learning the lesson of being stuck is so that the soul that has committed suicide realizes how their action has affected their family, friends, and even strangers. They have to learn that their lives matter. They must examine their life to see that there were other solutions besides suicide.

Usually, there is a time-lapse before the assistance of crossing over is provided by the other side to those who commit suicide. This is a part of the lesson, not a punishment. If the soul were taken to the other side immediately after committing suicide, it would not learn from it. Then that pattern would likely be repeated in the next lifetime, causing more misery to everyone involved. Interestingly, a soul who commits suicide does not attach to anyone (unless it is ready for help); it hovers in places that some may sense are haunted or have weird, spooky energy. The energy may feel sad, depressed, hopeless, and/or angry.

Ultimately, all spirits need to cross over to the other side. This is the natural process of a soul's journey. After crossing over, each soul goes to its appropriate level. It is like moving from city to city and returning to school. If you are a first grader, you continue into the first grade. If you are in a higher grade, you go to that grade. With a soul, it is the same. It goes into the appropriate soul level. Assistance is given according to the soul's needs. The soul can choose to come back as a guardian angel or a spirit helper until it decides to reincarnate again.

Note: Once all lessons are mastered and we become enlightened, we no longer have to return to Earth. However, many enlightened souls choose to come back to Earth life to assist in Earth's evolution. The soul has many paths to choose from.

REMOVING SPIRIT ATTACHMENT(S), ASSISTING SPIRIT(S) IN CROSSING TO THE OTHER SIDE

Cleansing Steps (CS)
Step 1 - Preparation
Step 2 - Removing Spirit Attachment(s), Assisting The Spirit(s) In Crossing Over To The Other Side
Step 3 - Chakra Healing
Step 4 - Activation of Self-Healing Green Color Energy
Step 5 - Activation of Spinning Points
Step 6 - Activation of the Universal Light

Begin with initial step 1 of CS found in chapter 9

Step 2 - Removing Spirit Attachment(s), Assisting Spirit(s) In Crossing To The Other Side

When dealing with an earthbound spirit, you must establish communication. It does not matter if you cannot hear the spirit if you sense its presence or feel some sensation. Speak out loud to the spirit like you would speak to another person. Explain what happened; explain to the spirit that s/he is dead and that it is time to join his/her family on the other side. You can also light white candles and tell the spirit that this light is for him/her to guide him/her on the journey to the other side.

Next, imagine that you opened a beautiful golden column of light and that this is a portal. This portal of light rises from the Earth and goes up to Heaven (to the other side). Call for your own family spirits to assist you in helping this soul cross over. Call upon the spirit's family members already on the other side to assist. (Everyone has someone on the other side waiting for them). Many times, the family from the other side will come to help you. It is easier for the spirits to trust you and cross to the other side when they see those loved ones waiting for them.

Keep the golden light portal open for as long as you need to in a session. Some sessions are quicker than others. You will most definitely sense it when the spirits decide to cross over and leave. You may see it in your mind, but if not, you can sense it. Usually, an incredible feeling of release comes over you and those still here and connected to this soul. You will experience feelings of peacefulness and serenity and love. Please tell your client that if the spirit desires to visit him/her, s/he can do that from the other side. Spirits LOVE to visit and help!

When you receive feelings of peace, then close the portal. Imagine the golden light dimming down and going back into the Earth. Thank everyone involved in the process.

When you are finished, continue with the remaining steps 3, 4, 5, and 6 of CS. It always feels good to reenergize the body with new energy.

AFTER – HELPING THE FAMILY

The time after a loved one dies is a very hard one. When you assist a spirit in crossing over to the other side, you will also have to help their family understand that their loved one is in a beautiful place, is happy, healthy, and, above all, a loving home, where they can do many, many things. Describe as many details as you can. Relate all messages, if any, and please use your intuition to help them through their grief. Remember, you are assisting earthbound spirits who still see everything from Earth's perspective. I do not deliver low frequencies or hateful messages or add anything to the message the receiver wants to hear if the spirit does not share it. If there is no message, that is fine; simply offer compassion and understanding. Help the family find ways to cope with the loss and avoid depression. Talk gently about stages of loss and grief that will take turns in upcoming days and months - denial, anger, bargaining with God, depression, and finally, acceptance run their course. After the acceptance, you can assist the family in finding their purpose and adjusting to a new life without their loved one being physically here. Be sensitive and compassionate.

When a person dies in this world, she/he is born in another world at that exact moment. As we mourn here, a grand celebration occurs on the other side— much like welcoming a newborn into your life.

My personal story: My grandfather passed away when I was 18. Every year on his passing anniversary, I became sad. My grandfather's spirit first assisted me in my conscious awakening. On his passing anniversary, he told me I should no longer feel sad for him. He communicated to me that it was his time to go, and instead of feeling sad for him, he wanted me to feel happy on the day of his passing. He wanted me to celebrate the day he was born again! At first, it felt a little odd to me. We are taught to feel sad when a loved one passes. But the truth is, our soul is infinite. It never dies. It just journeys from place to place. Our body is a temporary vehicle for the soul. So, allow yourself to feel sad for the departure of someone you love and rejoice in the knowledge that your loved one is continuing the journey somewhere else. And that somewhere else is a much better place than here!

CHAPTER 8

PAST LIVES

Past lives are the doorway to your ancient memory. They are consciously recorded in your Book of Life (Akashic Record) and your soul memory - which also contains your spiritual DNA. Your soul continuously projects your past lives memory as a hologram into your subconscious mind. Any unhealed past lives traumas may surface as perpetual issues in your current life and eventually manifest as unexplained pains or illnesses in your physical body. Past live energies just act out for attention.

Past life traumas are caused by unresolved past lives issues, emotional energy attachments, terrible deaths, and/or vows from past lives. Those traumas are like scars or bruises on the soul that cause a blockage, unhappiness, physical or emotional discomfort, anxiety, or even mysterious illnesses. Remember, scars remind us of where we have been. They do not dictate where we are going.

HOW DO YOU KNOW WHEN THE PROBLEM ORIGINATES FROM PAST LIVES?

We all experienced extraordinary past lives and traumatic past lives. We are consciously aware of our current life past but only remember something from our past lives. When diagnosing a problem, you want to find the root of it first. Once you know the root of the problem (and if this root originated in the past life), then you can release the trauma and heal the soul. Look at the pattern in your current life. Are you physically ill, but doctors cannot determine what is wrong with you? Are you controlled by unrealistic fears or anxieties? Ask questions like: Is there a reason for me to be sick? What am I afraid of? Is there a logical explanation for your fears or your illness? If not, your problems may originate from one or more of your past lives.

Past life energy is NOT classified as negative intelligent energy. It does not hide. It is the same in the present- and past-time reading (when you read energy 5 minutes in the past like you already learned in the chapter about mechanical implants). Past life energies are not waiting there to harm you. They are waiting for you to release them and move on with your life.

For example, you may have an unexplained fear of water, but nothing happened to you in your current life to cause this fear. What if you drowned in your past life? Your soul memory would encode the dread and terror you suffered before passing. Another example is that you may have unexplained digestive problems, and even doctors may be perplexed about your illness. What if you were betrayed or poisoned in one of your past lives?

I worked with a client who deliberately took poison to end one of her past lives. The emotional charge and sadness in her soul from that life were so strong that they followed her into her current life, causing mysterious digestive illnesses. Another client had uncontrolled guilt issues, fears, and over-protectiveness. One of her past lives revealed that someone very close to her died in an accident, and her physical body went into shock; this shock was imprinted in her soul memory. She felt so guilty because she convinced herself she could have prevented this accident by staying home rather than going out with her friends. The unfortunate accident was not her fault; however, for the rest of her life, she felt that it was her fault, and that feeling was imprinted in her soul energy. Unconsciously she carried these feelings of guilt, fear, and over-protectiveness into her current life. In her present life, she could not remember why she had these feelings.

The other sign that you may be affected by the energy from past lives is that whatever you do, you may have problems manifesting good things in your life such as finances, abundance, love, friends, and so on. Your past life reading may reveal that in some of your past lives, you took vows not to use your abilities, to be poor, to be celibate, unhappy, etc. Why you decided to take these vows may sound foolish now, but it was necessary for you then. In fact, it was so important that the energy of it imprinted itself onto your soul. Your soul manifests all your wishes according to your free will.

MEMORIES OF PAST LIVES

Usually, we do not have conscious memories from past lives. You may wonder, "Why can't I remember it all?"

Let's begin with ancient knowledge. You must lower your vibration when incarnating into your Earth body, depending on your soul evolvement before your current incantation. Lowering your soul vibrations causes loss in your conscious memory. When you spiritually awaken, you begin to remember tiny fragments of one or more past lives that are impacting you today: by experiencing strange dreams or having unexplained feelings. But you need to remember more to understand it all. From a holographic point of view, everything is there, all your soul's memories, but your conscious physical mind is not trained to access it.

Before you came to this body, you understood this, so you have prepared several triggering situations to help you remember who you are, your life purpose, and your past lives. The reason, the only reason for these triggers, is that you will remember who you are and remember your ancient knowledge. One benefit of healing your past lives is that you can regain all the skills and abilities you once had. When you consciously remember, you can heal and spiritually progress faster. Now, of course, you may wonder, if you can design triggering situations, why would you not have healed your soul in the above state when you had your whole soul's memory before incarnating. The answer is simple; it would interfere with your Earth soul's mission and your learning experience on Earth. What happens on Earth needs to be healed on Earth. That is the Earth's energy law.

For some people near death, experience is one of the triggers, a catalyst to gain some of the past life memory. This usually manifests itself as a life-changing event.

When babies are born, they still have a memory of their past lives. Unfortunately, they cannot share all their incredible knowledge with us because they cannot speak. When you look into a newborn's eyes, you can sense that they want to tell you so much, but they cannot express themselves in a way we can understand since we are not trained to communicate telepathically.

Many young children today can recall their past lives. Children tell astonishing stories that stem from their past life memories, and parents often think the children are just making up stories or that their child has a colorful imagination. When a child comes to you and tells you a story about a strange place, people, or animals s/he knows, just listen, and ask questions. Open a dialog and play along! Help the child to feel comfortable and develop trust. The doorway to the soul world may stay open instead of closed, and it is more likely that that door will remain open if they are not ridiculed or ignored. Many kids today can see auras, spirits, or guides. Does it mean they all have to become psychics and healers? Absolutely not! However, we must teach children to develop and utilize their unique abilities so that when they grow up, they will use them effortlessly in any job, and Earth will become a much better place with less greed and violence. Our children are the natural embodiment of Love and Light energy. While teaching them, we are making positive changes on our path and in their future.

READING PAST LIVES

Reading past lives is becoming a popular and widely accepted modality. When you nurture your unique abilities and start assisting others, you will realize that you can access past life memories. What can you do with this? Should you read past lives to gain intriguing information or offer more assistance, perhaps a healing? When you begin accessing past life information, you connect with your client's energy on a soul level. This is such an intimate moment, and your challenge is to bring healing to these past lives.

I pause for a moment and will repeat myself: you are responsible for bringing healing to the past lives but are not to seek changing occurrences in the past lives. The past cannot be changed, but it can be healed. Also, you are not just healing past lives. You are healing a soul! The soul of your client trusts you, has chosen you, and has shown you information for the purpose of soul healing and spiritual soul growth for both you and your client. You can access only information and past lives aligned with your client's highest purpose. Be honest in sharing what you see, sense, and experience, as this is a transforming experience, and someone may have been waiting for your assistance for a very long time.

How do I know the person who reads my past life is telling me the truth? How do I know what I sense/see is accurate and not just my colorful imagination?

It is simple. The reading must make sense to you and those you are reading for. Let's say I read for you and tell you that you were a soldier in 1800. If I am correct, this will make sense to you on some level. Most likely, you will be interested in that era and the military. You may reply, "Oh my gosh! That is my obsession!" The past is encoded inside our DNA. You may not recall it consciously, but unconsciously you are drawn to things and events from your history that is the same or similar in this lifetime. Even though you may not remember, your soul remembers it all.

I will often observe a significant injury, and a client will subsequently confirm that s/he has had unexplained pain in that part of the body for some time. The mysterious pain is the connection to the past and happens to help you remember. Another good example is the experience of a client I worked with who severely injured his leg in the Civil War. Not much help was available to him then, and we sensed that he suffered for a few days until he passed away in agonizing pain from an infection connected to the leg injury.

We returned to that lifetime during the Civil War, and I assisted his soul in understanding his passing. We released that lifetime's anger, agony, sadness, and desperate feelings. The pain (in this lifetime in his leg) went away as mysteriously as it came because we healed his soul.

Any traumatic energy from past lives can be released from the soul memory and healed. Past lives' soul healing is tremendously powerful energy work. It opens many doorways and memories into the ancient past. Before the healing is granted, soul trauma stands like a monster by these doors (into your ancient memory), intimidating you with fears and misery. It appears as the most fearsome monster you can imagine, and then, when you heal this monster and open the door, you suddenly realize there is nothing to fear. Fear itself is an incredibly powerful energy! Imagine each fear you have from this lifetime or past lifetimes you created to protect yourself from the trauma you already suffered.

Once you open these doors and understand your fears, you can start rekindling good memories and positive energy and perhaps recover abilities you had in your past. For example, suppose you were a healer, doctor, leader, scientist, mathematician, philosopher, builder, baker, etc. In that case, once you make a conscious connection and learn how to raise your vibration, you cannot relearn your crafts unless you deny it. Of course, the memory does not come back like magic overnight, but you can pick a book, study your favorite subject, and remember with surprisingly little effort what you knew in your past lives.

HEALING PAST LIVES

Cleansing Steps (CS)
Step 1 - Preparation
Step 2 - Healing Pats Lives
Step 3 - Activation of the Universal Light

Begin with initial step 1 of CS found in chapter 9.

STEP 2 – HEALING PAST LIVES

Healing past lives as described here is not hypnosis but conscious energy work. Conscious energy work carries tremendous healing power for the healer and client.

When you undertake past lives healing alone, please modify the steps for convenience and personal comfort. You have all you need (within you) to proceed with the healing. You should record each session so you do not need to hold each detail in your conscious memory, which would distract your work. Below I will describe a typical healer-client scenario.

When you suspect your client's problem may originate from past lives, you will prepare the client's energy for time travel. First, follow Step 1 in the CS, then briefly cleanse all chakras (energizing is unnecessary now). Just do a quick aura and chakra cleanse, as this will assist in removing the top layer of the energy so you can join deeply with your client's soul energy.

To prepare the soul to read past lives:

Put your hands on your client's feet (or close by since feet are part of the first chakra) and attune to his/her energy.

Focus your energy on your heart chakra and your soul, and consciously ask that your soul be connected with the soul of your client for the purpose of a past lives soul journey.

Ask your guides for access to your client's Book of Life (Akashic Record).

Take your time. Focus on your breathing. Take slow breaths and imagine slowing your energy down; everything is quieting down; everything is slowing down. If any thoughts come to your mind, just let them go. Become one with the emotional body of your client. The soul's energy is accessed from the emotional body.

Imagine that both of you are enwrapped in a beautiful pink glow.

To view past lives:

Fully trust that you are connected to your client's soul. Imagine that you are standing on a balancing beam and that you can easily navigate left or right. The center where you stand is marked 0 or a neutral point, the present moment. This is your current date and year. When you want to view the past, shift all your energy to the left. When you want to see the future, move your energy to the right. Please remember that when you see the future, you can only view it as probable since it is not written in stone. Now you will start with your client's current age and count backward (in your head or out loud). Returning to your client's past means moving to the left on your balancing beam. Let's say that your client is 50 years old, so you will begin 50-49-48 ... You can count year by year or in multiples of five or another number. It is great to acknowledge what happened last year or the year before—that way, you will establish a good connection, and your client will feel comfortable. Then you can count by 5s or 10s, whatever feels good. Stop at each age when you feel-think there has been some emotional charge signifying something negative happened. The energy may feel resistant, like you are pushing against a bubble. It is okay not to see what happened, but you may say, "I sense that something happened around your 30s. I sense sadness and blockage in the energy flow. Do you remember if something significant happened to you at that age?"

Acknowledge all the significant (unhappy) moments and continue until you sense that your client is a fetus in her mother's belly. You may like to identify the kind of pregnancy it was. Suppose the mother was unhappy to be pregnant. In that case, if she had significant physical or emotional difficulties during her pregnancy, your client has been carrying all this energy within his/her soul since he/she was in the womb. Often this is a sensitive topic, so be incredibly gentle and compassionate, demonstrating your understanding and caring when asking the client questions.

Then, spend a moment sensing the soul of your client as a warm, golden glow above his/her mother's abdomen before the conception. (You can often sense a soul in the mother's energy field up to three months before conception.) Recognize your client's soul and how s/he felt before conception; was s/he excited about his choice of parents? Why did he choose them? If you keep asking, the facts will emerge.

Imagine shifting even more left on your balance bean and asking your guides to show you the most prominent lifetimes affecting your client's energy. You may feel like you are just not getting through, but feelings, images, colors, and intuitive knowing will suddenly pop up. It is important to stay with it and persevere, and the truth will emerge.

Do not force anything; do not invent anything. Use your intuition and share what you see or sense in your inner mind. Allow years, pictures, symbols, and images to come to your mind, and share them with your client. You may get much information or just a little—all is perfect and in divine order. It may not make sense initially, but it will come together if you persevere.

You may also ask simple questions to help you determine what you are experiencing: "What do we need to learn from this lifetime? What caused emotional trauma in this lifetime? What caused happiness and joy in this lifetime? How did (name of your client) die in this lifetime? What did (your client learn in this lifetime? When you know all, you can and have a sense of completion, go to the time of death in that particular past life and see, feel, or imagine your client's soul as a golden glow rising out of the body and going up to that dark in-between space you have experienced before. You go there together because you are together on a soul-healing journey. You just let the soul guide you. You may repeat this scenario several times until you have learned enough for this session. (You may perform only one past life reading or several per session - this depends on you.)

Healing past lives:

When you sense you have seen all the lifetimes you need to see at this time (one lifetime is more than enough, sometimes less is more), you will feel a sense of completion. You will begin the soul-healing process. You will retrace your steps backward. Begin with the last past life you experienced in this session. Note the highlights of all that has happened. You already know how the soul died, the cause of death, and the cause of emotional scars on the soul. (The emotional scars on the soul are often the same as the unhealthy repeating pattern in the current life.) Without any judgment, try to understand what kind of life it was and what kind of person your client was. It does not matter if he/she was good or bad as long as desired lessons were learned. Made in our creator's image, we are all loved unconditionally. Healing happens by understanding life's purpose, accepting it without changing it, and forgiving everyone involved and oneself. Welcoming love of God's Source love in the end. Share this with the client periodically so there will be no shame or judgment, no matter what is revealed.

Finally, imagine a beautiful blue/white light extending from your soul (your heart chakra) into your client's soul (from your heart to your client's heart). Talk to the soul like you would talk to your best friend. Explain what happened and talk about how it is a normal part of life to pass away and that she/he will incarnate again. Help your client to make amends if any are needed. Assist him/her in releasing all guilt, worry, fear, anger, and pain. Healing happens by understanding life's purpose, accepting it without changing it, and forgiving everyone involved and oneself. Welcoming love and connection with God's Source (Oneness) in the end. When you feel you have accomplished this, send your blue/white light to the soul again. Send love, light, and healing so the soul can exist in other lifetimes (forward) with the best possible reality.

Repeat this step with all past lifetimes you have seen in the session. The description may seem lengthy and exhausting, but once you get the hang of this technique, it is fast, smooth, and energizing! To return, just think about the current incarnation, descend with the soul into his/her mother's womb. If your mom had problems loving you while pregnant, bestow yourself with unconditional love. Snuggle yourself in a blanket made of love. Be there at birth and go through all the years until the current date. You will feel like a blue/white fireball of energy returning to today.

When you are done, continue with step 6 of CS. Now you can enjoy a curious discussion on what you both experienced and accomplished.

I see about three to five lifetimes when I perform past life regressions. If I read for this person again, I would see different lifetimes as we will not need to see those we have already healed. The best advice I can give you on reading past lives is to believe in yourself and your abilities and trust the guidance you receive! All the information you access is released to you to learn, let go and heal the soul, mind, and body. Note: You can access only Akashic data for your client's highest purpose. There are many things you cannot control.

Here is example: All I could see was darkness when Rachel and I entered one of her past lives. (I like to keep my eyes closed and perceive pictures in my mind). At that point, Rachel's energy became very, very upset. She started physically twitching on my healing table, and her breathing became erratic. I could feel we had descended into her past life, but all I could see was dark! I could sense my guides telling me all was fine and to continue. Then I could hear in my mind, "Black Plague 14th century." As soon as I said that out loud, I became physically sick (a sign of making an energy connection in that time frame, but please know that not everyone experiences physical reactions), and Rachel was not feeling well either. I was holding her ankle, spinning points (add chapter). I felt sick, but intuitively I knew I should not pull away because we would lose this connection to her past life, and full release was needed. Rachel was lying on the healing table. With one hand, I reached for a chair close to me, sat down, and kept holding her ankles and energy connection. I shared out loud all I sensed, felt, and saw in my mind.

I could sense that Rachel was a man in the life we had entered. His family was already dead from the plague, and he was the only one left. He was still healthy (not infected) and decided to help others. He could leave the town, but he chose to stay and help. (I was sharing with Rachel all that I saw). The man went from house to house and helped remove sick people from their households. He took them to another place where they gathered the sick and cared for them until they died.

Eventually, he became sick as well. I could sense physically how sick he was and how terrible he felt. Luckily, I was sitting because I would probably have passed out if I had been standing. The interesting part was yet to come. When he (Rachel) was dying, he did not think about his physical pains. All he thought about was that he had failed. He was torturing himself because he got sick and could not help anymore. He did not give himself any credit for what he knew was a suicide mission. He saved the lives of many by sacrificing his own life to help and comfort those sick and dying.

I kept talking to Rachel's soul and helped her to see what a gift he was to his community and how many people survived because of him. This was a very emotional moment. Once it clicked in Rachel's mind in the current time, once she acknowledged it and understood it, the emotional energy was released from her soul, and the scar was healed. Rachel took a deep breath and released a deep, contented sigh. She stopped twitching and was lying peacefully on the healing table. The feeling of sickness disappeared, and we both felt good. This was the only life we accessed in this session.

In this lifetime, Rachel deals with problems by not allowing herself to be herself. She takes extreme steps to always please others and always puts herself last. Having seen how courageous she had been in the lifetime we accessed; Rachel gained the confidence to be herself. This remarkable accomplishment changed her life every day for the better.

NOTE: You notice that with Rachel, I referenced only one lifetime. The trauma of that life was so significant that I was guided to do only this one lifetime in this session. Rachel's nervous system had been weak for years. The healing needed to come in small increments to allow her nervous system to slowly heal and stabilize before another lifetime was accessed.

When healing past lives, read the past lives energy all the way through until you feel it stop. Then go back, life by life, and send healing to each life you have seen. Some need more energy and sharing, some less. Follow your intuition. Share all that you see. Explain to the soul what happened and bring peace and healing. Send light to each life you have opened and finish by sealing the energy. If you feel your client has several layers from past lives, you may design a healing journey for him/her. I like to do this in three to four past-life sessions, each a week apart. I put emphasis on healing and counsel on how to move forward with the life the client desires to have.

CHAPTER 9

CURSES AND ILL WISHES

Curses are as real as you and I. I was not a believer until I witnessed the effect of a curse. I am not an expert on this subject, but I want to share what I have learned.

Curses and ill wishes are a form of negative energy consciously sent to someone. Some people just curse you under their breath, and some go to more extraordinary lengths to hire someone to conjure a spell to send negative energy to you. Also, when someone speaks badly about an individual, he/she is projecting negative energy onto that person. The negative energy will affect the individual's personal energy and, over time, can make the recipient of the curse unwell.

When the curse or ill-wishing energy enters one's energy field, he/she will start unconsciously sabotaging his/her happiness. His/her mood can change as fast as the clouds roll across the sky. The recipient of the curse may feel irritated with people he/she loves or cares about for no reason. One minute the recipient may feel withdrawn from the whole world, and the next, will find the recipient acting out for attention. The curse recipient will often literally create drama. Why? The spell affects and steals his/her energy, and she/he feels energy-depleted, literally exhausted. S/he is acting out and unconsciously becomes an energy vampire, draining people who care about him/her. This may be very annoying or irritating to those close to the curse recipient, so they will withdraw from his/her life, and the spell is working!

I did not know much about curses until I moved into the Hispanic community in Chicago and began working with them. I am still astonished at the curses and evil thoughts people send to one another. The Hispanic community opened my eyes, and then I realized it was not just their community. Every culture employs this Dark Energy!

So, what is the curse, spell, badmouthing, or ill thoughts all about? It is energy. In the same way, you send healing energy; you can send harmful energy just by thinking toxic thoughts! Just as you ask angels and guides to assist you in light work, there are entities you can request to do Dark work for you. Is this right? Let me state that there are consequences to all our actions, Light or Dark. This chapter will focus on how to reverse or release this negative energy.

Remember that a curse is a form of energy. People use tools to cast a curse (blood, stones, ashes, bones, animal sacrifice, etc.), and strangely enough, some of these tools are the same props people utilize in sending a loving Light spell. These props are powerful because they allow and empower one's consciousness; the more you believe in them, the stronger the energy directed to you becomes (for either Dark or Light energy). On the other hand, not believing causes a blockage that weakens the energy being directed toward you.

When you think bad thoughts about a particular person or go so far as to conjure a spell on them, you consciously send negative energy toward someone specific. What happens next? If this someone does not know about energy protection, she/he will be energetically impacted on the left side of the body. (We receive energy from the left side, leaving our body through the right side.) First, the negative energy will affect the spleen meridian, making you worry because worrying will weaken other organs and the nervous system. Meridians are energy pathways in the body. They are the energy transportation system that carries this energy information into the entire body. Eventually, it will weaken the immune system, and the cursed individual may become ill, even extremely ill, depending on the strength of the negative energy directed toward him/her.

The basic rule of the curse is that the one who sent it wants you to know who the curse is coming from. They may give you a hint or send the energy intention that creates a sense of paranoia in you so that you start fearing that you may be cursed and begin to imagine and create stories in your head. All this is cleverly designed to take your personal power (or call it your personal luck) away. Once you start to fear, the job is done, and the curse is successful. This energy is similar to what you feel when you know someone dislikes or hates you. If you allow this energy in (by feeling bad, etc.), you empower it! If you give in to it, all this energy feeds on fear, unhappiness, misery, and emotional drama. The more fearful and miserable you become, the stronger the curse becomes.

I want to mention the critical importance of free will. The negative energy is sent, and you may get affected like you get caught up in a bad rainstorm. But what happens next depends entirely on your free will. Will you stay outside in the rain, cold, wet, and miserable? Or will you find a nice place that is warm and dry? Whether dealing with a curse or negative thoughts, will you react to the fears and confusion that the energy created? Or will you get to the bottom of why you are afraid and do something about it?

In my practice, I have seen some powerful curses that made people terminally ill. The sad part is that all this sprouted from jealousy, greed, and the need to be seen as better than someone else. All this ill-wishing is done by people who are angry, egoistic, selfish, jealous, greedy, domineering, and never happy (though they may think they are). Some curses take a different turn than designed initially, and instead of affecting the intended targeted person, the child of the targeted person may be affected. I have seen powerful curses and other curses that went totally wrong.

When you remove a curse, you do not return it to the one who sent it. It must be released and given up into the Universe for cleansing. Karma will deal with those who sent the curse. Even though we are a part of God's Source, we lack the power of God's Source to decide how those who sent us the curse should be punished. If you know this and still try to punish the sender of the curse, then you are no better than them. That is indulging in a battle of egos!

REMOVING AND HEALING CURSES AND ILL WISHES

Cleansing Steps (CS)
Step 1 - Preparation
Step 2 - Removing Curses and Ill Wishes
Step 3 - Chakra Healing
Step 4 - Activation of Self-Healing Green Color Energy
Step 5 - Activation of Spinning Points
Step 6 - Activation of the Universal Light

Begin with initial step 1 of CS found in chapter 9.

STEP 2 - REMOVING AND HEALING CURSES AND ILL WISHES

Scan the energy five minutes in the past (same as you learned in Chapter 4). Curses can also hide their energy, but they differ significantly from implants. You will feel possessive energy, and you will feel human energy connected to this possessive energy. You may feel bumps or lumps in the energy field.

Please note there is a significant difference between implant-controlling energy and curse/ill wish possessive energy. It is non-human energy vs. human possessive energy. A good example is a love curse.

While energy scanning Tony's body, I noticed he had bumps in the energy over his heart. I could sense that his heart was healthy, so the bumps did not result from an unhealthy organ. While sensing his energy, I felt his ex-girlfriend, and something did not feel right. We discussed that she felt jealous and was very controlling in their relationship. We also discussed his current marriage and the difficulties between him and his wife. The bump in energy increased when we spoke of his ex-girlfriend. You could literally feel the essence of her energy present with us. While we spoke of Tony's wife and their difficulties, the energy mellowed. After removing this negative curse energy from Tony's system, his relationship with his wife improved, and he felt much better.

If you suspect the curse or feel a bump or lump in the energy, or any other shape that feels possessive, neutralize the energy the same as you would work with implants. Then call for the assistance of Archangel Michael to cut the cords and energy links.

Cutting the cords and energy links:

Keep your hands over the neutralized area and say out loud or in your mind: "I ask you, Archangel Michael, to separate all energy cords and energy links away from (your client's name) that take away his/her energy and vitality. I ask that you remove all of the lower energies that reside within (your client's name) soul, mind, body, and energy field so that (your client's name) can attract new loving energies. I ask you to escort all these negative energies away from (your client's name). Thank you, thank you, thank you."

Next call is for Archangel Azrael, asking him to remove all dark and evil energy.

"I ask you, Archangel Azrael, to remove all the dark forces, energies, and entities and their implants from (your client's name) soul, mind, body, and energy field so that (your client's name) can walk on the path of Love and Light that she/he has chosen. Thank you, thank you, thank you."

Finally, raise your client's vibrations, fill him/her with unconditional love, and **continue with the remaining steps 3, 4, 5, and 6 of CS.**

After Cleansing

I suggest obtaining a piece of lapis lazuli for people who had a curse put on them so they can accurately see how things truly are and who is and who is and who is not their friend.

You can teach your clients how to protect their energy and use crystals, talismans, or any other energy tools for energy protection. The best protection against a curse is self-transformation, knowledge, and putting yourself on the highest available path. When you strive toward the light and start to see the good in people and become positive, negative people and negative energy will leave you alone because it will not thrive from you anymore!

PART II

CLEANSING STEPS

CHAPTER 10

CLEANSING STEPS

Step 1 - Preparation
Step 2 - Varies with each type of cleansing. Follow the detailed instructions described in each chapter. Note: exception for past lives reading/healing.
Step 3 - Chakra Healing
Step 4 - Activation of Self-Healing Green Color Energy
Step 5 - Activation of Spinning Points
Step 6 - Activation of the Universal Light

STEP 1 – PREPARATION

Before your client arrives (if you are doing a cleansing in person), or before you call, make the distant soul connection (if you are doing a distance cleansing), call for your guides, angels, God's Source (any or all whom you would like to join you in your cleansing energy work). Ask them to assist you. Ascended masters and archangels like to help in this tedious work alongside your guides. Also, call for the highest vibration guide of your client to participate. This is important because your client may have a low-vibration guide or someone who may just be pretending to be his/her guide. You just need to invite the higher-vibration ones. Since you have yet to learn what you are dealing with, you do not want to get involved and be tangled with an odd energy.

If you are doing a cleansing in person and will be using crystals, go ahead and set them up. I like to set crystals around the table and around the house in the following locations:

Client's Feet – grounding stones.

Client's Head – selenite and clear crystals pointing away from the table.

Client's Sides – a variation of fourth chakra crystals. My favorite is rose crystal on each side.

All the healing room doors and windows – black tourmaline and tiger eye. This helps stop negative energy from escaping. The implant will try to escape and find a new vessel.

When your client arrives (if you are doing a cleansing in person) or when you have made the call to make the distance soul connection (if you are doing a distance cleansing), help your client relax and feel calm. Have him/her rest on the healing table or meditate silently for a few minutes. Next, you ask to be connected with your client's soul energy. If you are doing distance cleansing, you may state your client's name and date of birth aloud to ensure soul connection.

Note: Unless you are doing a past life reading, do not attune yourself to your client's physical energy, only to his/her soul energy.

Next, open the connection of energy flow to the Axiatonal Grid (Torus field is part of the Axiotonal Grid that is a part of God's Source). The energy line connects the physical body's energy with the Earth and Universe. Stand by your client's feet, place your palms by the soles of his/her feet, and open Axiatonal Grid (torus field). Imagine a beautiful Atlantean crystal in the center of the Earth. Draw on its energy and bring it into your client's body. The silver energy will flow through you into him/her. It will connect with each of his/her chakras, entering by the feet. Then it will fill, illuminate and expand horizontally into the color of each chakra and leave the body from the Crown chakra. It will go upward through the Soul Star chakra and connect with the Universe. The energy will then return, traveling around the body, into the Earth, reaching the crystal, and coming back up. Do this connection about three times or until you feel you are done. Now, the energy system of your client is fully open and ready for the energy work.

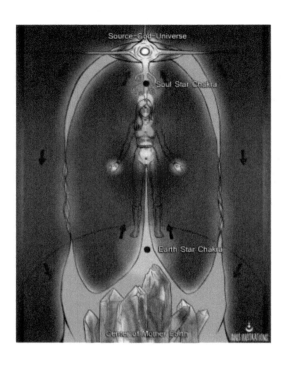

STEP 2 – VARIES WITH EACH TYPE OF THE CLEANSING

Follow the detailed instructions described in each chapter. Note the exception for past lives reading/healing.

STEP 3 – CHAKRA HEALING

After you finish Step 2, you are ready to work on bringing in new energies and activating new healing energy. You will be doing this with the help of the Lotus flower essence/energy. You will be working with opening and activating all seven chakras:

Muladhara - Root Chakra - Red
Svadisthana - Sacral Chakra - Orange
Manipura - Solar Plexus Chakra - Yellow
Anahata - Heart Chakra - Green
Vishuddha - Throat Chakra - Blue
Ajna - Brow Chakra - Indigo
Sahasrara - Crown Chakra - Violet

Note: You will repeat the following procedure with each chakra separately.

Start with your client's Root chakra (Muladhara). Imagine reaching into the essence of the red chakra with your hands, pulling a little red light out, and scoping it in your hands. Hold this light/energy in the palms of both your hands and imagine that it is a little lotus flower bud. Now shine/vibrate/channel your own healing energy and healing light from all sources onto your hands. You can also focus on energy from Ancient Atlantis to be poured in simply by thinking of it and making a mental connection. Imagine this energy/light filling the lotus flower bud - like a bright glowing sun and nourishing it until it blossoms into a magnificent lotus flower. When you feel you are done, gently place the lotus, filled with the vibrant red color, in your client's Root chakra, and put your hands briefly over the chakra (palms facing down). Imagine and state aloud or silently in your mind, "Red lotus flower activated." This brilliant red energy will thrive and protect your client's body energy for up to two weeks.

Repeat this step separately with the remaining six chakras, using the corresponding colors for each chakra accordingly. Make sure to send love, joy, and happiness vibrations with each lotus. This is enjoyable work! When you do this, you and your client will feel uplifted and filled with new energy.

When you finish the seven basic chakras, you will move to open the hands and feet chakras, respectively. You will open these chakras simply by setting lotus flower buds in them. Cup your hands together, as you did when channeling your healing energy and healing light from all sources onto your hands; imagine white light slowly filling the bud inside your palms. Like with the lotuses before, make this light grow into a beautiful white lotus flower. Then, gently place the lotus, filled with the vibrant white color, in your client's left-hand (chakra is the palm of the hand). Imagine and state aloud or silently in your mind, "White lotus flower activated." Repeat the steps three more times, placing each white light in the right hand, left foot, and right foot (foot chakra is on the sole of the foot).

When done with the hand and feet chakras, move to the Crown chakra (Sahasrara) to form a protective shield. Proceed gently, touching your client briefly in the middle of the forehead with your middle finger. Imagine a bright violet light on your client's forehead and state aloud or silently in your mind, "Violet diamond activated." The point of the middle of the forehead is different than the third eye. The third eye is located on the forehead between your eyebrows. Now, once you have activated the violet diamond point, imagine a violet light, like a beam, coming off the middle of your client's forehead - from the violet diamond point, connecting to the left-hand white lotus, then left-foot white lotus, right-foot white lotus, right-hand white lotus, and then back to his/her forehead, forming a violet shield around the body. This brilliant violet energy will spin clockwise and stay in continuous motion. It will thrive and protect your client's body energy for up to two weeks. It needs to be refreshed to keep vibrant. You can do this or teach your client to maintain this healing energy.

STEP 4 – ACTIVATION OF SELF-HEALING GREEN COLOR ENERGY

Activation of self-healing green energy is essential as a preventive energy medicine for your client to adjust to our society's unhealthy environment. Green is the universal healing light reflected in nature and healing crystals. It is the color of the Heart chakra (Anahata) and heart meridian.

Most importantly, green energy can be preventive medicine without unhealthy side effects. To activate it, place your hands, palms face down, upon your client's head and, with the assistance of your guides, visualize the vibrant green healing light coming down from the Universe, entering through the head (Crown chakra), and flowing directly into your client's body. Then, imagine and state aloud or silently in your mind, "Universal green healing light activated." The green energy will enter the head and proceed into the throat, filling your client's mouth with "liquid" energy. It will then follow down to the esophagus, lining it with its healing energy as it travels down into the stomach, creating a protective energy layer in the stomach organ in a circular motion. The energy will stay in the stomach. You can imagine it as a gooey liquid with a honey-like consistency. This healing energy will assist your client's body to soften the impact of illnesses from our food and environment. The Lights of the Universe created this procedure to help everyone develop healthy bodies because a healthy body aligns with and promotes a healthy mind and soul consciousness. However, please be aware that no energy can protect you against the self-destructive habits you may develop. You have to be willing to recognize them and be willing to heal them. Developing healthy habits that support a healthy lifestyle is highly recommended.

STEP 5 – ACTIVATION OF SPINNING POINTS

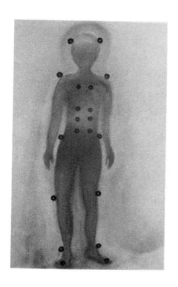

Spinning Points are small energy vortexes in our physical bodies. Most are located over bones and major joints. Our bones are part of the nervous system and produce bone marrow. Bone marrow is essential in cellular reproduction. Most importantly, bones, like chakras, store emotional, trauma, and negative energy. Once you start working with the spinning points, you will learn to move energy through your body and move it from the Earth, through your body, and out into the Universe. Doing this procedure results in faster recovery and rejuvenation. I strongly recommend teaching this technique to your clients so that they can do it whenever necessary, specifically when feeling stagnant. This is also excellent practice for starseeds to work with their unique energy.

Spinning Points are located on both sides of the body, and you must work both sides accordingly.

Locations:

Sides of the head (temples) – both sides

Shoulder joints – both sides

Upper chest – both sides (about 2 inches below clavicle bone and out to each side)

Lower chest – both sides (below the rib cage)

Navel – 4 points (2 on each side), about 1 inch above the belly button and out to each side, and about 1 inch below the belly button and off to each side

Hip joints – both sides

Knees – both sides

Ankles – both sides

Bottoms of feet (soles) – both sides (about 1½ inches below middle toe)

To begin:

Imagine energy coming directly into your client's feet from the Earth - like when you opened Axiotional Grid. State aloud or silently in your mind, "Earth energy activated."

Start at either foot. Place the client's foot between your hands with palms facing one another. You do not need to physically touch the foot. Then, slowly start moving your hands in clockwise motion, as though your palms are pedaling a bicycle. This simple moving motion will activate the electromagnetic energy in the spinning point. Begin slowly and gradually increase the speed, following your intuition. Do this for five to ten movements or until you feel you are done. Move on toward your client's other foot and repeat the process.

When done with both feet, move to the ankles, repeat the same process, one ankle at a time, then move to the knees, working on each separately.

When done with both knees, continue to your client's hips. Starting with hips upward, you will now work with both sides simultaneously.

Place your hands on the side of each hip, and create the same bicycling-like motion to spin the energy in the joints.

When done with both hips, continue to the belly - starting with two points below the belly button (as shown in the picture)

Place your hands, palms facing toward the first two spinning points below the navel. Spin them simultaneously, and let your hands move naturally, do not overthink this. (At these points, you are not sandwiching spinning points between your palms, instead, your hands move like you are rubbing your belly after eating something delicious.) Right-hand moves clockwise while the left-hand moves anticlockwise motion. (If your left hand is dominant then you can move left hand clockwise while right hand moves anticlockwise). Then repeat the same with two spinning points above the navel, lower chest (just below the ribcage), and upper chest (just below the clavicle bone).

When done, move to shoulder joints. Repeat the bicycling (rotating) motion with both hands, "sandwiching" the spinning points of both shoulders joins like you did with hips. When done with the shoulder joints, move on to the sides of your client's head (temple) and spin them simultaneously.

When you sense that you are done, smoothly pull all the energy above the head of the client and send it up toward the Universe. It is like you have taken an electrical cord from the Earth, wired it into your client, and then plugged him/her into the Universal outlet. Everything is connected and interconnected. Finally, imagine and state aloud or silently in your mind, "Universal energy activated. Spinning point connection complete."

Once these points have been activated, they can be used as cleansing points in your next session. You can cleanse spinning points the same way you would chakras, always in a counterclockwise motion. This is a great technique used not only for cleansing but also for any type of energy healing.

STEP 6 – ACTIVATION OF UNIVERSAL LIGHT

You are almost done. Now you just need to activate the Universal Light in your client and seal it. Therefore, you need to imagine a funnel of violet light (the Universal Light) coming down from the Universe into your client's body, entering through his/her head. Position your hands over your client's Crown chakra (Sahasrara) and guide all that light inside. This may take several minutes until you sense that it is complete.

Next step, imagine a golden spiral starting above the head and coiling around your client's body, ending way below his/her feet. You must then close the coil. You can also use a clear point crystal to draw the spiral surrounding your client's aura and then use it to also close the aura, preserving the protective field. Finally, imagine and state aloud or silently in your mind, "Auric field closed. Energy sealed".

After you have sealed the energy, you could fluff your client's aura. Starting at his/her feet, roll your arms one over the other and move them over the body from the feet to the top of the head about three times. This will feel very good and refreshing to both you and your client. Afterward, check your client's aura. It should be much bigger than before you started. Advise your client to keep the energy up and schedule a follow-up session. You may like to set up at least two follow-up sessions with your client just for energy healing to boost and rejuvenate his/her energy after a thorough cleansing.

After your client leaves, make sure you do your cord-cutting—quick energy release—by saying, "I want to release all the energy that no longer positively serves me. I want to separate all the energy cords and energy links from this session." Take a deep breath and release. Now say, "I want to release all energy and energy attachments attached to me during the session." Take another deep breath and release. Shine your soul light and then close your energy.

When you are done with all the steps, you may feel tired. This is long and tiring work, and it is acceptable for you to feel physically exhausted and emotionally drained. You deserve a good rest after any (and every) session.

PART III

REHABILITATION

CHAPTER 11

NEGATIVE ENERGY WE CO-CREATE

"The seed of light, the seed of love, and the seed of fear were all planted into human creation. Each seed requires nourishment to grow into a magnificent plant and thrive. Each plant generates new seeds that sprout with each season. Which seed are you feeding?"

Until now, you have learned about negative extraterrestrials, spiritual implants, psychic implants, abduction, past lives blockages, curses, and ill wishes. You have also learned the steps required to remove them and heal that part of your soul energy. Now you will learn about the rehabilitation of your energy and how to address the negative energy (fear) that you have unconsciously co-created over long periods to help you cope with everything happening to you.

It may sound odd that you have created a protective shield (made of fear). It often appears as another obstacle after healing, as you need more time to be ready and willing to set aside your protective shield.

You may feel initial energy high after the cleansing or negative energy removal session. This feeling may last approximately 1-2 weeks, and you may experience an energy downfall. Why? Realize that you have just removed something that has been with you (or your client) for most likely a very long time and that its removal has left significant damage to your nervous system and lifestyle. You were used to suffering, and now you may not even know how to live a happy life without any despair.

It is not much different than rescuing someone from decades of captivity. There is an excellent level of joy and a significant level of fear. One would need assistance to learn how to be free.

The same thing happens with your energy. You need rehabilitation. You must train your whole being to overcome the fear of being done with your protective shield, thrive again, and live a life filled with love and happiness. This can be done through spiritual inner self-work and transformation, spiritual coaching, seeking knowledge, meditations, energy healing sessions, etc., to rejuvenate the mind, body, and soul.

WHAT IF?

Often people spend a long time worrying, "What if the implant or spirit or curse will come back again? What if I get abducted again?" That "what if" generates tremendous fear of something that may never happen again. "What if" will lead you back to suffering instead of happiness.

If any of those things try to return for whatever reason, you already know what to do with it. Learn to understand your fear, and you will rise from that level of fear into a level of unconditional love where negative energy will not bother you anymore.

WHAT ARE YOU AFRAID OF?

I used to be terrified by many things. I was not afraid of death itself, but I feared "something." I was unsure what that "something" was, but I knew it was waiting for me. This fear stood with me for many years and followed me into adulthood. It was not until I started the spiritual journey that I realized that "that something" was just my fear that I literary manifested into a monstrous entity.

My fear started at about age two when my psychic abilities opened after an electric shock. This fear that began to manifest was gaining strength from several sources, including the current unhappy life with its many sad events, dramatic past lives memories, and not understanding my empathic and psychic abilities.

Fears have many origins but are just a program to protect your survival. Fear can quickly become your protective shield and can expand drastically. If you "baby" the fear and do not deal with it, the fear will eventually grow into anxiety, panic attacks, depression, or some severe illnesses.

Most starseeds could write a thick book about Panic Attacks, Anxiety, Fears, and Depression. (I will combine and refer to all these symptoms as the PAAFD monster). I used to suffer all these symptoms and know how hard it can be to overcome something that literally holds you down.

When I finally realized that the "something" I was afraid of was just a big glob of dark energy made of my fears, I was totally shocked. For many years I was convinced that "something" was after me. In reality, what was after me were my fears that I was trying to outrun, but they always caught up with me.

Take a little time and write a list of things you are afraid of. Nothing is too silly.

Example: darkness, people, spirits, losing a job, losing a house, being ridiculed, being unhappy, being alone, being sick, failure of life mission, failure as a wife, failure as a husband, failure as a mother, failure as a father, failure as a son, failure as a daughter, being abducted by ET's, etc.

1,

2,

3,

4,

5,

It is essential to recognize and name your fears.

Now take your time and write down the worst-case scenario for each fear you named. You can start to work with just one fear at a time. Write down all the details and remember that everything is okay and reasonable.

For example, let us use the emotional fear of the dark at night.

I fear the dark because I can sense all kinds of dark beings.

Next, write the worst-case scenario.

While I walk to the bathroom in the middle of the night, a dark portal will open, and a monstrous entity will jump out of the wall and kill me. In the morning, my spouse will find me torn into pieces and lying in a puddle of blood. The case will never be solved.

When you read this, it sounds ridiculous, but for someone with a fear of night and darkness, this scenario can trigger anxiety every night.

Now let us examine this fear and take it apart: In this scenario, you are afraid of the suffering of pain (most likely connected to torture in past lives) and, ultimately, the unresolved case of your death. Once you recognize this, the next step is to go deep within yourself and think, "Why am I afraid of pain and death?" Now try to rationalize it. If this monster comes out and does what I imagined, it may be painful, but eventually, I will die, and the pain will go away. My family will be upset, but I will be fine. My soul will leave this body and will embark on a new journey. I may not want to die, but if this scenario manifests itself, death will be the end of physical suffering.

In the bigger picture, you fear death and pain (not the darkness or monster) and must find a way to make peace with it. The fear is most likely connected to past lives.

Once you can logically reason with fear, the next step is to convince yourself to walk to that bathroom in the middle of the night and enter it with an "I do not care" attitude. Your heart may be pounding. You may be sweating and looking petrified to the wall, but it is YOU or IT. Just face it! It is just an energy monster and cannot physically harm you.

Walk in there and claim this area of your house. Put your foot down, stomp on the ground meaningfully, and fill this room with your soul light. If you can, send unconditional love to this monster. Declare that this is your space and that the monster has no business being there. Then when nothing comes out of the wall, take a deep breath, and acknowledge that you have stood up to your fear and are standing there safe, unharmed, and alive. Feel the release of fear and give conscious emotional feedback to your body that nothing has happened, and you are busy and safe. You may need to repeat this a few times until this new energy registers in your body, experiences a "mental click," and shuts this fear out of your life.

When you consciously know what you are afraid of and that it cannot hurt you, you create a "mental click." A mental click is a conscious understanding of your fears and will help make them disappear. It may take some work to allow yourself to create a "click," but if you focus your energy on it, release the old, and embrace the new, you will overcome your fears!

ANATOMY OF PAAFD MONSTER

Fears could make your creative mind go insane. You will develop many possible scenarios that Alfred Hickok would be proud of you. Living constantly in these possible fearful scenes eventually leads to anxiety, panic attacks, depression, or severe illnesses, and the PAAFD monster is born.

The PAAFD monster is manifested by your own energy and will become your protective shield, so you will never spiritually grow because it falsely thinks it is keeping you safe. It will need a lot of negative energy to feed on, so it can grow, thrive, and keep you miserable.

Once you manifest your PAAFD monster, it is hard to break from its grasp. Sadly, many starseeds believe that they are insane, that something is mentally wrong with them, and that they are just stuck. If you can think consciously about what you are experiencing, and see that this is not right, if you are searching for answers and help, then you are on your way to beating the beast and getting your life back on track.

Before I continue, I also would like to point out that anxiety, panic attacks, fears, and depression often trigger awakening points for many starseeds. As bad as it may seem, and as much you may not like it, feeling bad makes you search for untraditional forms of healing. More than likely, it also brought you to this book. Most starseeds suffer from being oversensitive to traditional medicine, food, and the environment. For that reason, they are more determined to find something else that will work for them while they continue their journey and find their true self.

Many starseeds eventually realize that this is a lesson, an opportunity to understand their own energy within their body. Cleansing your soul of negative energy is one thing. Understanding how your energy works, who you are, and why this is happening to you is another. Once you understand what is triggering your nervous system and what your fears are, you can face your fears and use this knowledge to protect your energy and develop your abilities to serve you positively instead of making you sick. Just this realization makes your "monster" much weaker!

VICTIM

Be aware that your PAAFD monster will want to make you feel that you are the victim so that you can feel sorry for yourself and create more low energy for him to feed on.

"Do not be a victim! Be the boss!"

When your fears arise and your anxiety creeps up, the best thing to do is NOT TO GIVE it what it wants! And as crazy as it sounds, accept it and change it. Changing takes some time, but it will happen once you start working on it and take the necessary steps.

"Take your power back! IF and WHEN are procrastination words. DO and CREATE right now."

AM I A PSYCHIC VAMPIRE?

Usually, when you become a victim of the PAAFD monster, it will demand more and more energy to feed on. The PAAFD monster lives on negative, angry, highly charged, unhappy emotional energy.

Without knowing it, you may become a desperate psychic vampire to receive some "life energy." A psychic vampire is someone who steals energy from others. I do not want to cast a bad light on psychic vampires, as there are ethical psychic vampires, but this chapter is not about them. This chapter is about those who steal energy and cause emotional drama to get more emotional energy to feed on.

These poor people often do this unconsciously and are unaware of the problems they are causing. Please know that there is a significant difference between being possessed by a spirit or controlled by an implant than it is being energy-depleted and becoming a psychic vampire.

When you are energy depleted (and do not know how to receive energy from nature), you unconsciously seek anyone willing to listen to you and who will feel sorry for you. Someone who will empathize with you. When you finally find someone like that and share your drama and problems with them, they feed you with their energy as they listen and empathize. This makes you temporarily feel good and sustains you for a short period. Eventually, no matter how positive or understanding the others are with you when they become energy drained by you, you will translate that as meaning that they do not understand you. That they do not know how bad it is to be you. Unconsciously, you take their energy and sponge it in, but the monster is never satisfied. It wants more. The monster wants drama, chaos, and misery. The monster does not want a solution or just positive energy. The PAAFD monster will make you as miserable as possible, so you will, in turn, make the people who love you feel agitated, to the point where they explode and release their energy for you to feed on. If they get angry, mad, furious with you and "lose it," that is the energy that your PAAFD monster loves (this is not what you consciously love or want). This energy satisfies the monster, not you. It does not even make sense, right? And the circle continues until you say: "Enough is enough!" It is hard to stop being a victim, but it is harder to live the rest of your life as a victim.

Unfortunately, if you allow this to continue and do not change, the ones close to you who are trying to help, your wife, husband, girlfriend, family members, friends will feel extremely emotionally drained. They will start believing that you only want to "complain." They will not see your dark reality as you do, which will be very frustrating. Your complaints about your feelings drain them and make them tired. They are helpless. They would like to help you, but you discard everything they suggest because you do not like their suggestions and ideas, or you find an excuse for why it may not work for you. In their opinion, you make excuses for everything. In your opinion, no one understands you.

Making an excuse for any suggestions or ideas is procrastination. Procrastination is another form of fear.

Be selective about who you share your energy with. Learning how to open and close your energy, protect your energy shield, protect your own energy from sponging everyone else's problems, and cleanse yourself of unwanted energy is helpful. It is all energy, and you are the master of it. With a good energy routine, perseverance, and a strong desire to change your life, you will eliminate the PAAFD monster for good!

Mary And John

This is an example scenario to help you understand how the PAAFD monster operates.

Mary and John were going to visit mutual friends. John suffered for about two years from a fear of being among the people. The fear manifested as depression, severe anxiety, and panic attacks. Mary and John were fully aware of John's fear as they consulted medical professionals. They also searched for a holistic approach to help heal John's emotions and were learning to understand the concept of emotions and how they control us, especially fear. Mary supported him during his healing process, and both agreed that Mary would not emotionally feed his fears as they would never leave.

John began to feel overwhelmed at their friends' house and asked Marry if they could leave. Mary did not want to go but supported her boyfriend and left with him.

She was calm, but John was already upset, and it made him even more upset that she was so calm about the incident. He really needed her to feel sorry for him. On an unconscious level, his body needed and craved this energy from Mary to feed his fear monster, like a child would want a piece of candy to calm a tantrum.

146

It became challenging for Mary to stay calm and composed and not react to all his complaints and insults.

John was feeling worse and worse and felt like he would explode. Anxiety and panic attacks were building up. He experienced heart palpitations, sweat, mental confusion, etc.

If you were John at that moment and could feel his body, you would feel the surge of very nervous energy. It may feel like tsunami waves crashing against you as you try to live your life. If not recognized and healed, you may feel hopeless and believe that there is nothing in the world you could do to stop this except just give in and scream, yell, be mean, cry, or hide. You would do anything that you feel will make you feel better. This is a terrifying and dangerous experience.

As mentioned above, Marry and John had a conscious agreement that when John gets into his fears, she will be supportive but calm and quiet so she will not feed the monster. John must face this emotional feeling alone and realize he can overcome it.

Now let us analyze the above scenario. What really happened to John when he went to visit his friends? Why did it trigger his anxiety, and how could he have changed it?

John is a starseed, and each starseed is an empath. Each empath needs to learn to protect his energy. When John visited his friends, he did not protect his energy field. (He did not close his energy.)

Upon entering the house, John's own open energy acted like a magnet, and he unconsciously sponged on other people's problems. Since John lived in a lower vibration of fear, he empathically sensed everyone's inner fear. You feel and attract the energy you hold. That was the first trigger.

John did not realize that what he was emotionally experiencing was not his feelings but other people's. For example, if someone in the room felt low and self-conscious about their body, it amplified John's feelings because he feared being among people and was already worried about what they may think about him. Then, when he plunged into worry about what people think of him, the fear of being among people multiplied and consumed him. This depleted his already low energy and triggered his anxiety. Inside, he became furious and asked Mary to return home with him.

John forgot about the prearranged agreement they had. The monster took over. He did not care if he complained, insulted her, or yelled. The monster wanted to trigger Mary so that she would react back. If Mary had worked up her emotional energy and became mad at John and started to shout at him, insult him, etc., she would give her energy to him, which would satisfy John temporarily. This would fulfill John's monster, but it would make Mary sad, and the circle they were trying to break would repeat.

I remind you that this kind of action must only be when there is an agreement on both sides. Fears, anxiety, panic attacks, and depression are low-vibration energy. It does take time to cleanse them all and heal completely.

John eventually learned to recognize the pattern of his energy. He learned to distinguish between his feelings and other people's feelings. And with practice, John could control his energy by consciously opening and closing it. He took control and faced his fear. Once John was able to do this, all the symptoms of anxiety, panic attacks, and depression slowly left him as he was not feeding them any longer.

Summary:

Change the way you think. When you change the way you think, you change your energy pattern and your life. This can be done by facing your fears and consciously acknowledging your desire for change.

Be willing to take steps toward your new future. It has to be you and only you who will make the changes. There is a lot of help to assist you on your journey to a better life, but you are the creator of your future and need to become a doer of that future.

Research what may help you. Learn energy work. Research about appropriate herbal supplements, mineral deficiencies (this is a significant factor in mental health), healthy diet, and healthy lifestyle. Learn techniques on how to protect your energy. Please note that spiritual advice is not meant to supplement professional medical help. If you feel you need medical assistance go and seek it.

Leaving is acceptable if you find yourself in a relationship and feel that you cannot help the other person and become victimized. You can help only those who want to be helped, and you need to take care of yourself first.

You are the only one who can make changes in your life. You have all the tools you need.

CHAPTER 12

NEGATIVE ENERGY AND DARK BEINGS ATTACKING ME WHILE I SLEEP

During your awake hours, you are working on your conscious spiritual journey and may be experiencing bliss and joy throughout the day. At night during your sleep, you experience terrifying nightmares. When you wake up in the morning, you are exhausted, perhaps scared by the explicit content of your dream, and sometimes even discouraged from pursuing the Path of Light. I hear this often from many of my clients.

Let us begin with free will. Everyone is saying that we have free will, but what does it mean, and how does it relate to your nightmares.

In your physical life, your free will is greatly limited by your society, the rules you must follow, and your choices. If someone comes and physically attacks you, your free will does not exist at the moment. You will desperately need to use your physical power to protect yourself, call for help, or do anything to save yourself.

When it comes down to most of your personal life choices and the invisible energy world that surrounds you, which is composed of dark and light energy, your free will has incredible power because you have free will to choose how you FEEL. The dark side does not want you to have this knowledge because if you figure it all out, the dark side will weaken.

The dark side feeds off your fears. It does not want you dead, as it may suggest in dreams. It wants you to be alive but terribly horrified for the rest of your life because that is what they thrive on. They want you to be scared, frustrated, and angry from the difficulty of your daily life, and at night they feed the fire with their nightmarish scenarios. You are sweating in fear and gasping for air while they are having a big party at your expense.

Once you consciously embark on your spiritual journey, or become conscious of living a more positive life, mindful of the food choices you make, mindful of your environment, etc., and start to question your life as to why you are here and how can you be in service to humanity, you become a bright light for yourself and a temporary red light for the dark side. Now imagine that when you are born, your light color is grey. Since the Earth realm is a place of duality, you have great potential to be either dark or light or both. Once the soul incarnates here, both sides enter the race to influence your soul to choose a side. The dark "ego-centered" with their fear tactics or the light "soul-centered" side with their unconditional love.

Unfortunately, each soul must cross the River of Forgetfulness before entering the Earth (very few souls avoided crossing this river) to forget who you really are. That is why you do not have conscious memories of your past lives.

The dark side does not control everything; fortunately for you, it cannot do anything to you on the energy level against your free will. Free will is a law that even the dark side has to follow. So once you become a bright light, it knows that it will be hard to corrupt your conscious mind, so it will intimidate you in your sleep. They also like to pretend to be your mystical, spiritual guide to keep you under their control. That is why everyone needs to learn to test their energy.

While you sleep, your body rejuvenates, and your soul travels astrally. Often the soul on the Path of Light likes to go to astral classes and gather knowledge so it can slowly guide you on your journey through Earth life.

Of course, the dark side does not like that, and it will test you to determine if your fears can control you. You may dream those reptilians (or others) attack you and experience insane violence. If you wake up scared, unsettled, and questioning everything you have come to know in this lifetime, then this is not just a dream, and you are under psychic attack. Did they target you specifically? The answer is no. They attack anyone who has become a bright light but still has some sense of fear. Their purpose is to keep you in a state of fear, at least in your astral body, so you will never fully awaken and be in service to humanity. These beings or energy can read you like a book. They will know what scenario will instill the most fear in you and will play "that movie tape" for you while you sleep. For some, it may be reptilians smashing someone, and blood is everywhere. For another, it can be an alien abduction. For someone else, it can be the death of a child, etc. They pick what you most likely will fear the most.

If you work, for example, a lot on your computer, they may show you that they know everything you do. They will make you feel like they control every step of your life. They are trying to instill in your mind that you have NO free will, are trapped, and that you better give up now.

If these beings wanted to kill you in your sleep, they would do it. They are just playing with you.

Perhaps these horrible nightmares will repeat a few times, and when you keep repeating something, it will eventually stick, and you may become paranoid in your awakened state. The power of belief has tremendous power. You will start reading and viewing videos about conspiracies, and they will begin to make sense to you. This will install a robust program of fear within you, and you will be stuck and under their control. You may still enjoy a happy life, but you will be significantly controlled by the dark side.

For brave people who do not fear the astral plane, the dark side may trick you into engaging in battles and wars. They will make you feel that you are an indispensable warrior. They may bestow upon you all kinds of weapons, making you feel like the leading hero in the most amazing video game you have ever seen. Some beings will approach you and express their gratitude for you saving them, and eventually, some will tell you that you are saving the Earth and that the future of humankind depends solely on you. Your human ego will grow beyond proportions, and even though you may be very spiritual, your ego will push you to be the one who knows it all. Unfortunately, this is also where you become stuck. These spiritual battles give you a false sense of accomplishment and spiritual growth, preventing you from reaching your true soul growth.

Think about it, life went on before you became the leading hero of these battles, and life will go on if you would not join them. We all want to be a superhero; the dark side knows this and will use it to inflate your ego and give you what you want.

WHAT CAN YOU DO?

You need to face your fears. As described in this book, write down what you are afraid of and why, and explain the worst-case scenario this fear can cause. Realize that none of this happens during the day while you are awake and only at night while you sleep. The best tool against these beings is to shine your soul's light and send them unconditional love. I know it sounds too simple, but truth be told, the power of your soul, light and unconditional love is your most potent weapon.

If you wake up in your dream (lucid dreaming) and there is a reptilian threatening you, send him your soul light and surround the poor creature with unconditional love because we all come from God's Source of unconditional love. The poor being has forgotten that. If these encounters happen in your dreams (in the energy world), this being will leave you alone, and you will most likely not have any more problems with him or them again. Hypothetically, suppose a physical reptilian is standing in your room, and you are not dreaming. In that case, you need to physically run or do anything you can to save your life, as this is an entirely different scenario that will take a whole other book to explain.

Remember, the free will law applies only to the energy world, to your emotions.

OTHER KINDS OF DREAMS

Once you are on your spiritual journey and working on reprogramming your emotions and behavior, addressing your fears, going through ego transformation, etc., you may experience unsettling dreams such as being lost, failing in something important, experiencing scenarios of being ashamed and feeling guilty or hopeless.

There is a simple explanation for this. What you release from your conscious mind is trying to re-root itself in the dream state. Think of it as if every part of cellular memory you work so hard to acknowledge, understand, and release so healing can take place is like a weed in your garden. You have to pull it out several times (from personal experience, it takes a few times to release some old patterns), and then it will test you.

Example: You may be working on releasing the shame from being abused, and suddenly, you start to experience dreams where you wake up naked in the middle of school or in a crowded shopping mall, feeling quite ashamed and upset because everyone is looking at you. Or you may be working on your self-confidence for a work promotion and will dream that you were flying an airplane and crashed and killed the whole crew. There are gazillion scenarios that may pop up in your dreams.

When this starts happening, instead of becoming depressed, get excited. This means that you have pulled a lot of weeds out of your garden, and they have become threatened that they will not be thriving in your garden anymore. This is their last attempt at re-rooting themselves.

In these dreams, you have the power of your free will. Change the outcome and make it work for you. Change it with unconditional love, not with your ego. Give yourself what you need. If you are naked, give yourself clothes - you are healing the pattern of shame. If you are failing at piloting the plane, then remind yourself that you are the best pilot out there (even if it is not true) – you are healing the pattern of failure. If you are poor, give yourself an excellent opportunity to earn money – you are healing the pattern of abundance. It does not have to make logical sense what you do in your dreams to change it, so it ends with a positive outcome, as long as you do it with unconditional love.

You can become a conscious part of all aspects of your energy. In your daily life, energy work and the work you do while you sleep. Fears will keep you as an obedient servant. Your soul wants to be free and will gladly guide you on your journey.

PRACTICE FEELING OF UNCONDITIONAL LOVE

Helpful to use while you are learning to overcome your fears or feeling lonely, gloomy, uninspired, etc., and when connecting to God's Source.

Quiet your mind for a few seconds.

Put your hands over your Solar Plexus and feel the energy of your 3rd chakra. Imagine you have a yellow flower bud inside.

Now, in your mind, imagine something you genuinely love. It can be anything. Let us use chocolate as an example. Now bring that beautiful feeling of your love for chocolate from your mind through your throat, heart, and into your Solar Plexus. Combine the imagination with the feeling. Now give your yellow flower bud all this love and see it blossom. Its petals are opening, and its beautiful yellow color energy fills your whole being with the power of inner strength and universal, unconditional love so you can do anything you put your mind to. Take three slow deep breaths in and exhale the air out. You feel calm, centered, and confident.

Stay in the moment. Trust yourself. Take a deep breath, and when you exhale, say, "I am the embodiment of unconditional love."

CHAPTER 13

A HEALTHY BELIEF

A healthy belief in yourself should be the second thing you learn on your spiritual journey after learning to open and close your energy.

It is human nature to believe in something. When you lose your beliefs, you may feel your life has no meaning and enter a self-destructive phase. That is why so many people turn to different religions, cults, even spirituality, or anyone who will listen and give them hope that there is something better waiting for them to ensure a light at the end of the tunnel. Sadly, many of these religions, cults, and even spiritual leaders, gurus, and teachers use their message and your need to believe in something to gain control over you and manipulate you. They use fear tactics to have you under their control. This is why the Lights of the Universe often speak about a healthy belief in yourself and free will.

Everyone has heard the saying that "If you truly believe you can heal anything in your body." It is also well-known that when you believe in yourself, you can accomplish anything you want.

Your physical body has self-healing abilities. You just need to learn how to gain access to the activation button or how to use it. Is that simple? Yes. And how is it possible that it works for one person and not for the other? The healing begins with believing. Whether it is healing from the effect of dark energy or a crippling physical illness, believing is the key to recovery.

Miraculous healings have been documented all over the world. I have met many people who have stumped doctors by overcoming various illnesses diagnosed as incurable. These people that miraculously healed all had one thing in common. They all believed that they would heal and recover. They prayed, did energy healing, holistic healing, traditional medicine healing, or nothing at all, but they all accepted the illness and believed they were healthy. Their rational mind was not in the way, and their body was in synch with their mind and spirit. They wanted it so bad and believed with all their heart that it was possible to heal, and instead of living in the future "that it will happen," they started to live in the present. They had empowered their belief in healing by feeling and genuinely believing that it had already happened, causing the healing to manifest.

Believing in yourself, your decision, and your actions open many doors to new possibilities. If you believe in good things, good things will happen to you. If you believe in bad things, bad things will happen to you. That is the way that the law of attraction works.

Believing in yourself means that you are embracing your personal power. It means utilizing your unique energy within and allowing your healthy confidence to awaken. You do not need to blindly follow someone else's beliefs. You can be influenced by and learn from them, but before following them, you should process the information through your energy system. Ask questions like, "Does the message strongly resonate with me? Is the message inspiring or fear infused?" Do not be afraid to be yourself, to create your own opinions, and to believe in your own decisions.

HEALERS BELIEF

It may sound surprising, but so many great healers have this doubt that no one wants to discuss. "Am I a good healer? Is my healing energy good enough? Am I really giving healing energy, or is it just my imagination? Do I really have the power to heal?"

The answer is "YES." Suppose in your heart you feel the call to be a healer. In that case, you can be a healer and possess beautiful healing energy that will allow you to connect with the healing energy of the Earth, nature, and the Universe for treating yourself and your clients. You just have to believe in it.

While working with healing energy, you rarely get the opportunity to see the actual energy doing its work, but you have to have faith in all you do. Some have the gift of seeing energy, but most people I meet feel the energy as it passes through the body. Just because you cannot see it does not mean it does not exist.

I will share my doubts about when I first started using my healing abilities. One day I stood with my hands above my client, silently thinking, "What in the world am I doing?" In my mind, I knew the steps I should take. I felt the energy, but not as strongly. I sensed my guides, yet I wondered if this would be enough. Then I telepathically heard my guides telling me to let go of my worries and believe in myself. And I thought, "What?" I heard it again, "Believe in yourself right now, and believe you are a channeler of healing."

I was thinking, "How will this help me right now?" What I wanted was an ultra-superpower right now. Well, I did not receive the superpowers. Still, because I trusted them, I followed their guidance, and at that very moment, I let go of the "Eva persona," who wanted miraculous healing to happen according to her, and I stepped into my higher self who had no needs or wants from the outcome of this healing. My mind chatter stopped, and I was one with energy. The energy that flew through me was powerful. It felt like a nice breeze was turning into a wild wind. I was amazed at what just simply believing could do!

WHY DOES NOT EVERYONE HEAL?

Everyone who embarks on the path of being a healer I have met so far has that original excitement that he/she can heal anything. If Jesus could heal by touching someone, why cannot you also? Your healing success may last for a while, and then you come across a client that, no matter what you try, will not heal. This could make you rethink your healer's path and stop believing in yourself. It may even lead you into depression. You may wonder if you are a healer; should you not have the ability to heal everyone? The answer is no.

Every healing originates on the soul level. Every soul has made a soul contract before descending into the Earth realm. When someone comes to you for healing, this person will heal only if the soul is ready, and a lesson was learned from that suffering. For example: One with an implant needs to know about acceptance and forgiveness, forgive those who placed it in him/her, and acknowledge that the implant was taken on a free will agreement to save someone else.

You can assist your clients in healing on the soul level by finding the root of the problem and guiding them to connect with it so they can let it go.

Believe it or not, even Jesus did not heal all people. There are three categories of people who will come to you for healing, and the success of the recovery depends on their willingness to be healed.

Miracle healing – Occurs to souls ready for a major transformation. Even though these people may need several sessions, they progress dramatically every time you work with them.

A few examples from clients I worked with A cancer patient healed and became a healer. A client who had shingles healed because she was ready to let go of her quilt that her brother had passed away when she was six years old (it was not her fault, but she believed it was). Another client experienced unconditional love after the removal of an implant.

Temporary Healing – This healing has occurred, but the symptoms and conditions return. Some people want to heal but are too scared to change. Every healing you do requires 50% participation from your client and 50% from you. If your client is open to healing but not ready for the change, then temporary healing may result, and sooner or later, the problems will return. This is why consulting with your client during and after the healing process is helpful and essential. In this way, you can ease your clients' minds and guide them through any issues they may have during their journey's transformation.

Jesus would work with these people, but along with the healing, he would teach and share ancient wisdom with them so they could find their way to full healing.

A good example is someone who is struggling with alcohol addiction and has failing kidneys. This person comes to you for healing, and you can channel enough energy into the kidneys to rejuvenate them. So this person has an excellent chance to change his life and save his kidneys. But if he convinces himself that it is okay to drink only on weekends and not every day as he used to, this is not enough for a transformation to occur. The choice is in the hands of your client.

People in this category of healing are like wild cards. They are too intimidated by change and often blame the healer (or anyone else) for the healing not occurring. These people need to find failure in someone else, so they do not have to face the fact that they, themselves, are failing to embrace a life change that will allow them to live a better life.

Healing does not work – This applies to those who simply think that they are entitled to healing, it must work for them, and there is nothing they need to change about themselves. Do you recognize the ego? The ego does not want you to heal and will not allow the client's soul to connect with you; thus, no matter how amazing you may be, the healing is not happening. Jesus would refuse to heal this kind of person.

If someone is disrespectful to you, demands from you, and tells you exactly what you should be doing to heal them (if they have this knowledge, then why do not they just heal themselves), or if they quilt you into healing them, this is a good sign that there is something wrong. These people need to open their souls and work with their egos before healing can work on them. You do not have to turn these people down, but you will have to adjust their healing into self-healing guided steps. You can guide them through the process but do not cater to their needs or allow them to take advantage of you because if you do, they will drain every ounce of your positive energy, leaving you weak and frustrated.

On your journey of healing others, you will meet people who miraculously recover, those who will progress at their own comfortable pace, and those who will not heal. You probably started your journey bright-eyed and excited that you would learn everything about healing and that you would heal everyone who sought your assistance, and then you realized that you can heal only those who are ready to be healed. You must keep your faith in everything you do and believe in yourself. There is a reason you were called to be a healer, and many people are waiting for your assistance.

You have to learn to respect someone else's wishes, even if you see they are not suitable for them. You can give advice, but ultimately you have to respect where others are in their soul growth and readiness for change. If you hold unconditional love for humanity, that is more than anyone can ever ask for. Unconditional love makes it much easier to respect someone's choice of not learning, not changing, and even not healing.

BELIEF AND EGO

There is a difference between believing in yourself and ego-based behavior.

It becomes second nature when you believe in yourself and feel comfortable with all you do. You will have no need to force it on others. Only the ego does this. It is fine to share your beliefs and knowledge with others and teach your ways, but the one who will learn from you must create their own belief. It does not matter if it is precisely the same as yours or different.

You can show and teach your way, but you cannot force your beliefs on others and insist that only your idea is correct. If that happens, we are back to the controlling ego and can compare this to something we have already witnessed in history, when religions used to force their beliefs on others.

When you can create and live by your own beliefs, you grow beyond the limits that someone can set. The best true teacher you can find is the one who encourages his/her students to become more than he/she is. If you can put your pride and ego aside and help others become more than you are and not feel jealous, then you are on the right track. Life is not a competition. Human life could be a very joyful experience.

CHAPTER 14

REBIRTH

After each major release, healing, or life lesson mastering, you are given a chance for rebirth. You can release the person you used to be and become who you always wanted to be. During your lifetime, you may have several rebirths. Small ones or big ones.

In some cases, just before the rebirth, you may feel tired, scared, and discouraged since it may feel like you will physically die. The human aspect of yourself is not aware that you are going through spiritual rebirth. Humans thrive in patterns, knowing what to expect so they can be safe. Many humans live in constant fear of something because being afraid serves as a safety cushion for possible failure.

The old issues you worked so hard to change could temporarily resurface again, bringing all kinds of old emotions, anger, and sadness to help remind you of what has happened in the past. Remember, you have already dealt with all of this. You went through cleansing and healing. You had mastered healing these emotions when they tried to re-root in your dreams. So why are they returning?

They are returning to test you one last time. Are you ready to let go of who you used to be? Can you relate to all these "old energy events" with a new positive approach? Are you serious about your change? It is just a test, and this test is easy to pass. If you stay within your new energy, all resurfacing will clear up as fast as it manifests, and you will be ready for rebirth.

You may also experience frustration, anxiety, and mood swing because, once again, your human is afraid of change. It is good to practice self-love and honor your feelings. You must also learn to recognize and change those feelings into their opposite so they will not get the best out of you but help you to create the best you can be. You are getting ready to lose a part of you that you know so intimately. You had good days, and you had bad days. You loved parts of your old self, and it is all ending. It is normal to experience the classical five stages of loss and grief. Do not get lost in them.

Denial and isolation
Anger
Bargaining
Depression
Acceptance

Atlanteans, Egyptians, Mayans, and Essenes have all practiced conscious rebirth. It marks the end of one journey and the beginning of a new one without physical death. It will save you a lot of time compared to a physical passing where you have reincarnated, regained your memory, and started your mission. With rebirth, you can take a shortcut and pass all of that.

169

Honor all your feelings, and instead of feeling stuck in the five stages of loss and grief, try to envision how you can move forward into acceptance. You have already mastered every step that has led you to this stage in your life. You are almost there.

Look at your life honestly and review all that has occurred until now.

Do not feel sorry for what happened. Understand and learn from it, so you do not have to repeat the same lessons. You want to start a new life pattern with a new soul mission. For example, if you have been controlled by an implant, it is time to truly step into your higher self. Take the last opportunity to release all that no longer positively serves you. Then, when you accept all this, you will be ready to start working on your new self and get to know yourself all over again.

Who am I?

What do I like to do?

What are my passions?

What are my desires?

What is my soul mission?

How can I be in service to humanity?

Am I happy?

Am I healthy?

Am I abundant?

Am I connected with my soul family on Earth?

If your new purpose is, for example, to create a new business, you can ask questions like:

How can my business be in service to humanity?

When you are ready, mediate and jump off the precipice. Embrace your rebirth and become the one you always wanted to be! Become the new you who is the embodiment of love and light frequency and always strive to be in service to humanity.

CHAPTER 15

YOUR GALACTIC TEAM

This is part of your story written in the books of Akashic records. Many of you were summoned to meet in the Pleiades long ago. Some of you lived there and called Pleiades your home while traveling from far-off star systems. No matter where you came from, when you hear about the Pleiades, your heart swells, and tears form in your eyes because your soul remembers the place filled with love and happiness.

Every one of you has a story about how you came to Earth. Many of you came to Lemuria and Atlantis and then left. Some of you stayed a little longer and have memories of civilizations in Sumer, Egypt, the Himalayas, Southern America, and other places. Everyone who feels connected to us and all these places has spiritually ascended at least once. Still, you keep returning to Earth of your own free will because you think you can be of assistance to bringing knowledge to humanity.

ZION, ALCYONE - PLEIADES

Warriors, inventors, scientists, doctors, healers, peacekeepers, planet developers, history librarians, and other experts arrived in space vehicles in anticipation of finding out why they had been summoned by the

Council of Light to meet on Alcyone in the Pleiades star system.

The brightest souls, the bravest souls, some awkward, some loved by all-star beings, misfits, rebels, bookworms, divas, beings with all kinds of backgrounds, looks, and personalities who did not necessarily want to associate with one another, had been invited to the most sacred place on Alcyone. They were asked to come to Zion, the City of Gods.

Some walked in groups and others alone as they made their way into the forest on top of the mountain where the entrance to Zion was located. Some have silently wondered, "Why have these others been invited? Surely, it must be some sort of mistake."

When they reached the gate, they were astounded by the megalithic structures that rose before them. They had heard stories of this place, but words could not describe the splendor of its presence. The site was constructed of light blue and white stone and surrounded by a misty white glow. A feeling of unconditional love transformed into silent peace when they approached the gate. They were welcomed by the gatekeepers. Everyone was asked to show his symbol of the light, written in their hand but invisible to the naked eye. They were then instructed to place their palm over their heart to ensure their symbol matched their soul frequency. The frequency match granted them access to Zion.

Zion, the City of Gods on Alcyone, is the oldest place in the Pleiades and surrounding planets. It is the sacred place of the elders across the Universe and home to the Council of Light. Those called to serve on the Council of Light are thousands of years old. They are tested and then carefully chosen before they are welcomed and invited to live in this magical city.

Those living in Zion are part of the collective consciousness. They are disconnected from all needs and desires, even from unconditional love, and live in infinite peace (which is a higher vibration than unconditional love) so they are not influenced or corrupted by others while making decisions for the beings of this Universe. The Council of Light residing in Zion are not Gods. They are elder extraterrestrial beings who witnessed and participated in many changes. Even the other star beings do not call them Gods, but they are highly respected and honored as they hold within the pure essence of the highest energy. Each could join with the oneness (God's Source) but chose to stay and be in service. They do not use fear, nor do they manipulate to get their points across. Their decisions are purely based on being fair and impartial, as fairness and impartiality are both neutral energies that provide equal treatment without taking sides.

The group of star beings gathered at the Temple of Wisdom. The building looked like a massive amphitheater. The Council of Light sat at the long semicircle table centered on a raised stage. Behind them, tall columns were raised up to the ceiling and sectioned off various entrances that led to other parts of the building. The architecture was ancient, solid, and massive. All the star beings were in awe as they sat in a semicircle, amphitheater-style seating. It was an honor to be there, and the anticipation of what would come next was intense.

Then the Council of Light spoke:

"Welcome beautiful beings of the Universe. First, thank you for accepting our invitation to meet here. We know it is unusual to gather in Zion as the standard is for us to conduct our meetings on your individual planets. But for what we would like to ask of you, we agreed that it would be better to show you much we love and honor you by inviting you to sit and be equal with us here in this most sacred place.

We are older than you and may have had more experiences because of our age, but on the soul level, we are all equal, and just because our experiences may be broader, this does not mean we are any better than you.

Our job is to keep peace in the Universe, oversee the laws we agreed upon, and assist in moving us all forward in our soul evolution until we are all connected again to the oneness of all.

The soul's journey is a joyful experience, but sometimes, as you know, the soul can become trapped in different realms. It can become lost, controlled, and dominated by those soul energies who still believe that only dark energy is the way.

We summoned you here today because we would like to ask for your help with Project Earth."

A little unhappy grunt was heard in the audience.

175

"Each of you asked to attend this meeting has already been on Earth. Whether it was in Lemuria, in Atlantis, or later. Each of you has mastered the ability to work with the human ego and embraced the energy of the duality of dark and light. Each of you learned to remember your soul star energy, ascend, and return to your galactic home. We know that Earth has not become the heavenly place we all envisioned at the beginning of this experiment and that it has become a training ground for new souls mastering soul-mind harmony. You know that many of our star brothers and sisters keep returning to Earth to assist all these souls in finding the same knowledge that allowed you to remember who you are and return home to us. In this way, the souls on Earth may one day find their way back home.

The Earth is moving into an advanced technological age, as Atlantis was once. They have been re-discovering new energies. Sadly, many still believe that every great power or energy should be weaponized and used to control others.

Earth beings are separated by many factors, and we ask you to enter another incarnation or series of incarnations to help them unite. To assist them in understanding these new energies and their positive advantages if appropriately utilized.

Just as the whole Universe is evolving, so is Earth. More power and ancient technology will soon be available to them. With that, they will also have access to ancient wisdom and teachings, but the hunger for control and power seems more potent than the hunger for ancient soul knowledge and ascension.

We did not ask one specific chosen group to assist them. We kindly ask you from different walks of life, backgrounds, and upbringings to re-enter the Earth incarnation cycle, incarnate in other parts of the world, and into different families. We hope that if you return and teach by example, the humans will follow and gain the knowledge necessary to reveal who they are. By sending such a diverse group of beings, you will be able to blend in amongst the different people of Earth. This will also guarantee various interests. Some of you will choose years of studies and become doctors, scientists, politicians, etc. While others will prefer to become street smart and self-taught and going to teach humanity that background and education do not define who you are or what you can accomplish and that it is the essence of your being that defines who you are.

We ask you because you all walk on the Path of Light. Even though you are different, you are unique, and each has something amazing to offer. You live with honesty and integrity, and you are the embodiment of truth and love."

An Orion warrior sat quietly in the back and felt slightly uncomfortable as others around him gleamed with light and pure happiness at the recognition. He preferred to walk alone. He thought it was no one's business to know he had a good soul and walked on the Path of Light. He wanted to keep that secret, but now as he looked at all these beings around him, he knew there was no point in hiding anything. He had learned about the dark side, embraced the light side, and knew that if you can unite those two elements, you will create a potent energy of oneness. He sensed he could be helpful on this mission to Earth, so he accepted it.

"We all know this mission will have many drawbacks, especially completely forgetting who you are. Those who like to think they control the Earth are not eager for us to come and assist humanity. Upon learning of our mission, they may bully you and traumatize you. So, we ask, will you accept this challenge?" We leave the decision entirely up to you and will fully respect it if you decline. We want you to know that some of us from the Council of Light will also take this journey with you. We would not ask of you something we would not do ourselves.

We will create units of healers, psychics, and consciously awakened individuals who can assist you in adjusting your soul-mind energy and fully aligning it with the physical body you select. It will be up to you to choose what you would like to do while on Earth as long it is aligned with our mission to assist humanity in the great awakening and evolution.

We ask you to be frequency holders. Remember the passion you have for what you do right now. May it become an infinite light that will feed your creative fire and allow you to hold that frequency and inspiration for others. When one awakens into the energy of unconditional love, one craves to be creative, helpful, and expressive, but one needs to be entirely on the Path of the Light. The dark side knows this and will try to scare, intimidate, and stop progress. When the light steps into the dark, its light will not be diminished. Only fears can do that. So, when the light learns to look into its fears and see them for what they are, the darkness is not scary anymore and could become a safe and protective shield."

The Orion warrior smiled because he knew what the council was talking about. He used to be so afraid to step into the light for fear that he would become less than a warrior and would drown in the puddle they called love. He smiled because he could not imagine that he once believed in that. When he walked into the light, led by his soulmate, he became stronger than ever. His wants and needs were gone, and unconditional love became his new compass.

He still enjoyed his weapons and a good fight with skilled opponents in a safe environment (the same as you would play football. Killing for fun was long gone. When he had to fight, he did it to protect those who could not defend themselves. He was stronger, better, and more content.

He thought about his life on Earth. In Atlantis, he was there with his soulmate. He would now have to take that energy imprint back to Earth to assist others in uniting dark and light energy. His triggers would be a difficult childhood, an unhappy love life, and discontent at his workplace. That is his specialty. He would also have the urge to have his own business, and all this would lead him back to remembering the essence of the brave warrior he is. He knew that the Earth realm would challenge his dark side, and he would have to work extra hard not to get corrupted with greed, need, and wants.

He smiled and thought, I can do this. If they are all going, even some of the members of the Council of Light are going, I am in. He loved a good challenge. He thought, "Life in the Universe is never boring." He slowly stood up and walked toward the elders facilitating the contracts for those returning to Earth.

Others followed him.

The next step for each volunteer was to return home to enlist close family members and friends who would be their galactic team while on mission Earth. Each of you has a galactic team eagerly waiting to work with you. They are your soul family, your fans, and your best supporters. They will communicate with you telepathically and energetically through numbers, symbols, colors, reoccurring events, and dreams. Things will happen to you or occur at specific times in your life. Just remember, there is no such thing as a coincidence. Everything happens for a reason, and your galactic team works behind the scenes with you. To connect with them from Earth, put the palm of your dominant hand over your heart, connect your heartbeat with the essence of your soul, and say, "I am here. I am ready. I am ready to work with you." Learn to communicate with your team and allow them to guide you.

Everyone sent down to Earth again is blessed with good luck. That is what we can do for you without breaking Cosmic Law rules. You are protected and will always find the help you need. It is up to you to accept it or not.

Everyone is trained in various healing modalities to heal and rejuvenate their bodies, mind, and soul.

Everyone is blessed to be abundant with all they need. However, unlimited abundance will open after the ego is mastered and controlled; otherwise, one would misuse the abilities as the human ego is easily corrupted.

Everyone is surrounded by unconditional love. Unfortunately, only some can feel it, as the Earth's realm is dense. It does not matter if you awaken or not or if you succeed in your mission; everyone is cocooned in unconditional love. No one is judged, and everyone is appreciated.

Farewell on your journey!

and

Welcome back to Earth!

CONCLUSION

I hope that the knowledge you gained in this book will empower you and assist you on your healing journey and the healing journey of others. When one aligns oneself with ancient teachings, the transformation follows. Be gentle with yourself, practice self-love, and believe in yourself. Trust that you can do this! You were born to do this! Always move forward, and never let negative energy stop you. Remember, you can always call upon the guides, The Lights of the Universe, to assist you.

I had been thinking about my final words for months when I finished this book. There are many ancient memories I would like to share with you, so instead of writing the last words, I will write another book!

Thank you for who you are, and I cheer you on your journey!

Love and Light,
Eva Marquez

ABOUT THE AUTHOR

Eva Marquez – The Pleiadian Whisperer is a spiritual consultant, soul healer, teacher, and writer with Pleiadian starseed ancestry. In her spiritual work, she utilizes her Pleiadian energy. Eva remembers the Language of Light along with many other ancient soul memories. She works with her guides – the Lights of the Universe- a collective group of light beings from various star nations (Pleiades included). Eva and her guides assist starseeds in remembering past life memories on Earth and beyond, activating their sleeping cosmic DNA, and connecting them with their soul family.

Eva's mission is to help starseeds adjust to their human bodies to carry out their life purposes to assist humanity in becoming a multidimensional race and preserve Earth for future generations. The alignment of the soul, the ego/mind, and the body is achieved through soul healing. In her teaching, she guides her students to prioritize understanding their feelings and the basic senses before thinking and acting. This results in self-discovery and self-mastery, where you can become your healer and guru. The body is a microcosm of the macrocosm. The chakras, the meridian, and the nervous systems act as cosmic highways within the human body. Eva's healing sessions explore those highways and their possible blockages.

Eva brings the memories of infinite love – the essence of God's Source – the most profound energy that is your original essence. She walks beside you on your life journey, assisting you in letting go of your fears of darkness and limitations and seeing the light at the end of the tunnel. Ultimately, she guides you to the point where infinite love is no longer a memory but your guide. Infinite love will become your friend on the journey toward the light of your origin. Love and light give birth to the wisdom that is a compass for the soul-mind consciousness on the healing journey of returning home to its original source. It is Eva's greatest wish that you find your way home.

Learn more about Eva and her services at
www.EvaMarquez.org

OTHER BOOKS BY EVA MARQUEZ

Activate Your Cosmic DNA: Discover Your Starseed Family from the Pleiades, Sirius, Andromeda, Centaurus, Epsilon Eridani, and Lyra

Pleiadian Code: The Great Soul Rescue

Pleiadian Code 2: Cosmic Love

Pleiadian Code 3 : Alien Fragment

ONE LAST THING

If you liked this book, I would be grateful if you could leave a brief review on Amazon. Your support means a lot to me, and I read every review. Thank you for being so supportive!
Love and Light,
Eva Marquez

LINKS:

Step 1 artwork (Opening Energy) and Grey Loom alien portrait was created by AIRIS Illustrations. You can find AIRIS on Instagram ashleyhinze_art

Printed in Great Britain
by Amazon

44121988R00109